2/7/8

D0734600

Demco, Inc. 38-293

Idella Parker

Idella Parker

From Reddick to Cross Creek

Idella Parker with Bud and Liz Crussell

University Press of Florida

Gainesville » Tallahassee » Tampa » Boca Raton » Pensacola » Orlando » Miami » Jacksonville

Illustrations are courtesy of Idella Parker, unless otherwise noted.

04   03   02   01   00   99   6   5   4   3   2   1

Library of Congress Cataloging-in-Publication Data
Parker, Idella.
Idella Parker : from Reddick to Cross Creek / Idella Parker ; with
Bud and Liz Crussell
p.   cm.
Includes bibliographical references.
ISBN 0-8130-1706-8 (acid-free paper)
1. Rawlings, Marjorie Kinnan, 1896–1953—Friends and associates. 2. Rawlings, Marjorie Kinnan, 1896–1953—Homes and
haunts—Florida—Cross Creek. 3. Parker, Idella—Friends and
associates. 4. Women domestics—United States—Biography.
5. Women authors, American—20th century—Biography.
6. Women—Florida Biography. I. Crussell, Bud. II. Crussell, Liz.
III. Title.
PS3534.A845Z842   1999
813'.52—dc21   99-31361

The University Press of Florida is the scholarly publishing agency
for the State University System of Florida, comprising Florida
A&M University, Florida Atlantic University, Florida Interna-
tional University, Florida State University, University of Central
Florida, University of Florida, University of North Florida, University of South Florida, and University of West Florida.

University Press of Florida
15 Northwest 15th Street
Gainesville, FL 32611
http://www.upf.com

*This book is proudly and affectionately dedicated
to my grandnephews*

Michael Mills

Jonathan Bowen

Jerrold Bowen

Justin Bowen

Garrett Johnson

Chalan Gadson

Jason Everett

Wade Tyson

Alva C. Brown II,
in memoriam.

Alva C. Brown III

George Prime

Edward Prime

Contents

Preface

AFTER PUBLICATION of my first book, *Idella: Marjorie Rawlings' "Perfect Maid,"* I received stacks of letters from readers wanting to know more about my experiences with Mrs. Rawlings. Many, many friends and fans have urged me to write another book, telling more about my life, my family, and my times in Reddick and in Cross Creek, Florida.

I have attempted to do that in this book, *Idella Parker*. You will be told more of my many memories of the experiences of my life with Mrs. Rawlings. You will also learn more about me, my hometown of Reddick, my family, and my heritage. You will read of my memories of Mrs. Rawlings' second husband, Norton Baskin, and the people I knew at Cross Creek. I have included pictures of my family, Reddick, and Cross Creek. I hope you will enjoy this journey to the past.

Acknowledgments

EVERY TIME I was asked to speak to a group about my experiences with Marjorie Kinnan Rawlings, people would tell me I should write a book. While I am a gifted talker and storyteller, I found it difficult to effectively handle a manuscript. I needed help getting my story together. So after a long time speaking to various groups I would end my talk with a plea for someone to help me. After one such talk sponsored by the Reddick Library Club, a Reddick schoolteacher came to me and offered to help me. That is how my first book, *Perfect Maid*, got started. My thanks to Mary Keating for that.

I can't even recount all the happy days I have had since I became a member of the Marjorie Kinnan Rawlings Society in 1988. When I was asked to be a speaker at the first three-day convention held in Gainesville, I didn't know what to expect. I called my niece, Marcia Johnson, in Pompano Beach, and asked her to go with me. We were the only blacks at the meeting, and I was nervous, but some of the members invited us to join them at their table, and soon we felt right at home. When we went out to Cross

Creek for the afternoon, Marcia sang for the group. My thanks to Marcia for her moral support.

Since that first convention, I have attended every one, and made countless friends from all over the United States. Some of my dearest friends from the MKR Society have also been my greatest supporters. I want to recognize Gordon Bigelow, Phil May, David Nolan and all the others for their advice, help, and kind words during the writing and publication of my first book, and now this one.

Many thanks to all my many fans for the kind letters, phone calls, and invitations to schools, clubs, and other associations. Thanks to the news media for helping me promote my book with pictures and articles: the *Ocala Star-Banner,* the *Gainesville Sun,* the *Jacksonville Times Union,,* *Fort Lauderdale Sun Sentinel, Miami Herald, Orlando Sun,* and all the many others.

A nice article was written about a talk and book-signing event I had one afternoon at the Seven Sisters Inn in Ocala. The news reporter, Bud Crussell, now retired from the *Ocala Star-Banner,* offered to help me after hearing me say I would soon start another book. When he finished the first draft of this book, his wife, Liz, a public school teacher in Marion County, came to his rescue and worked with me on the revisions. My thanks to both of them for helping me put this book together. I am well pleased with the way they have come into my life. Again, Liz and Bud, thanks.

Special thanks also to Dr. Kevin McCarthy of the University of Florida English Department and Rodger Tarr, Illinois State University Distinguished Professor, for the encouraging comments and valuable suggestions they made as readers of my latest manuscript.

My only regret is that my older sister, Hettie, didn't live to see this book in print. She passed away on October 7, 1998. She had recently made the statement, "I tried to live as Christ would have me live. I have had a grand time living." I can certainly say the same and hope that my story demonstrates it.

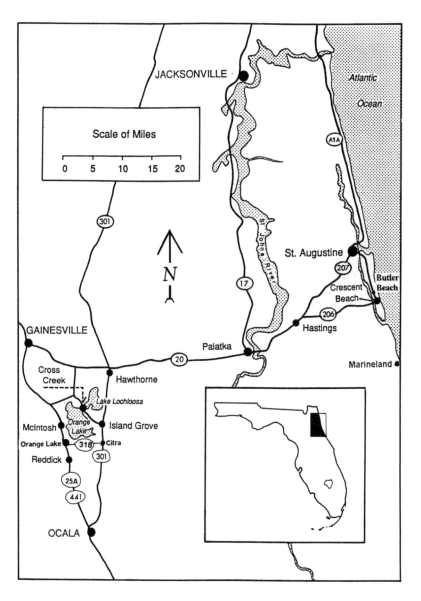

Northeast and Upper Central Florida

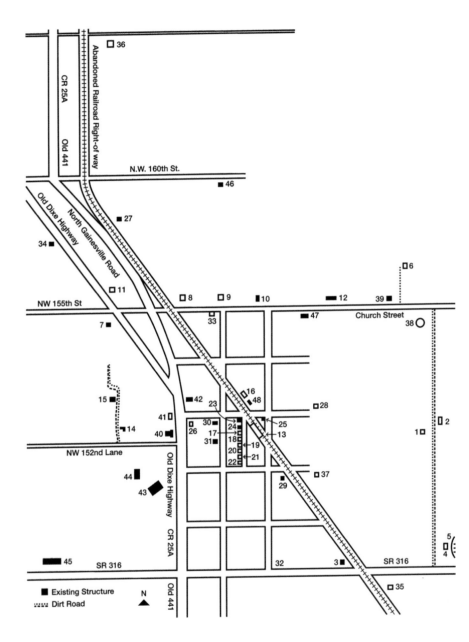

CR 25A
Old 441

Abandoned Railroad Right-of way

☐ 36

N.W. 160th St.

■ 46

North Gainesville Road

Old Dixe Highway

Old Dixie Highway

■ 27

34 ■

☐ 11

NW 155th St

☐ 8   ☐ 9   ■ 10   ■ 12   39 ■

☐ 6

☐ 33

■ 47   Church Street   38 ○

7 ■

15 ■

☐ 16
48

42 ■   23

☐ 28

41 ☐

40 ■

■ 14

30 ■   25
24   13
26   17
18   19
31 ■   20   21
22

☐ 2

1 ☐

NW 152nd Lane

44 ■

43 ◆

Old Dixe Highway

CR 25A

Old 441

37 ☐

29 ■

5
4
☐

45 ■   SR 316

32   3 ■   SR 316

☐ 35

■ Existing Structure   N
⋯⋯ Dirt Road   ▲

Reddick

Town of Reddick
Map Key

1. Site of Idella's birth house
2. Site of Aunt Hester and Uncle Hyman's house
3. Papa Ephraim's house (old Reddick house)
4. Site of Uncle Adam Turner's cabin
5. Site of Turner's Pond
6. Site of Papa Jake's house
7. United Missionary Baptist Church (site of Mt. Cello Missionary Baptist Church)
8. Site of Mt. Olive Baptist Church
9. Site of Masonic Hall
10. Mt. Zion United Methodist Church
11. Site of Mt. Zion Elementary School
12. Former Collier Elementary School (black)
13. Site of the Reddick Depot
14. William Cabbaris's house
15. Matthew Hart's house
16. Site of Dupree's boardinghouse and store
17. Devore/Yongue house and site of mercantile
18. Site of John General's meat market
19. Site of Rou's dry goods store
20. Site of Papa Ephraim's market
21. Site of Smith's mercantile
22. Site of Fridy's dry goods store
23. Doctor's office and drugstore
24. Reddick State Bank
25. Newer rock jail
26. Site of Mrs. Gutherie's store
27. Peter Brown's Hall
28. Site of old wooden jail
29. Judge Cromartie's house
30. Reddick Presbyterian Church (white)
31. Methodist Church (white)
32. Mt. Cello Cemetery (site of original Mt. Cello Baptist Church)
33. Site of ice-cream parlor
34. Club Charmant
35. Site of the Lime Kettle
36. Site of the Side Camp and turpentine still
37. Site of the Section Houses
38. Site of Mr. Mayo's Silo
39. Mama and Papa's house
40. Mr. Fanelli's house
41. Site of Redding's Ford Garage
42. Reddick Supermarket (site of Mr. Fanelli's vegetable shed)
43. Former Reddick School (white)
44. Reddick Public Library
45. New Reddick-Collier Elementary School (integrated)
46. Idella and Bus Parker's house
47. Thelma's house
48. Little Rock Post Office

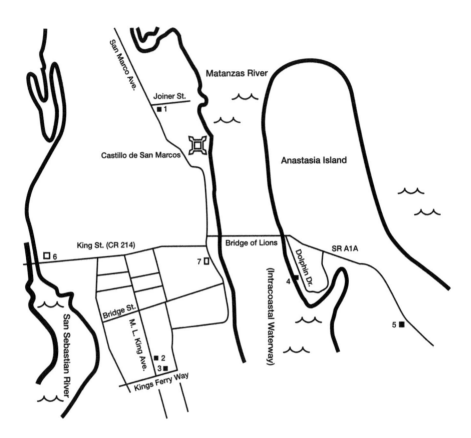

St. Augustine Map Key

1. Castle Warden Hotel (Ripley's Believe It or Not Museum)
2. 139 Martin Luther King Avenue (rooming house where Idella first lived in St. Augustine)
3. 81 Kings Ferry Way (Bernard's mother's house, where Idella lived after their marriage)
4. 77 Dolphin Drive (Mr. Baskin's house)
5. Alligator Farm
6. Site of Florida Normal College
7. 159 Marine Street (site of Flagler Hospital)

CHAPTER I

Idella

WITH MY humble beginnings, I certainly never set out in life to be a public figure, and even after the years I spent working for the renowned author Marjorie Kinnan Rawlings, it never occurred to me that anyone would be interested in my life. It was only after a news reporter for the *Fort Lauderdale Sun Sentinel* visited my classroom of educable mentally handicapped students in the early 1970s, learned of my past, and wrote a newspaper article about me that people suddenly took notice of me.

My principal brought her to my class to write a story about what I was doing for the mentally handicapped. My students were misbehaving, and the only thing I could think of to settle them down was to ask them if they had seen the movie *The Yearling*. Many had, so I said, "Did you know that I used to work for the lady who wrote that story?" The students were fascinated as I started to tell my story, and they kept asking more and more questions. When I was finished, the reporter told me I should write a book about my experiences.

Idella speaking at the Marjorie Kinnan Rawlings Society Convention in 1994. Photo by Phil May.

After her article came out in the paper, in which she told about my relationship with Mrs. Rawlings, I started getting calls. People from all over Broward County wanted me to come and speak to their groups and classes. My public life had begun; this story is about how my humble beginnings led to it.

I was born Idella Thompson in Reddick, Florida. Reddick is a little town about fourteen miles north of Ocala, the Marion County seat. Before you can understand much about my family's beginnings, you need to know a little about how Reddick got its start in Marion County, for the two are linked from that early time. Marion County was formed in 1844, shortly after the last of the Seminole Wars. The United States Congress passed the Armed Occupation Act as a means to entice settlers to the area. Thus began a land rush that brought wealthy plantation owners from the Carolinas to develop plantations in Marion County. With them they brought slaves whose work it was to clear the hardwood forests of this central Florida highland and plant crops. Large cotton and sugar plantations were developed north of Ocala in the 1850s.

Papa and Mama seated at home in Reddick in 1960.

Set in the heart of this beautiful rolling plantation land, Reddick grew up, as many other small towns did, along the newly laid tracks of the Florida Southern railroad. John M. Reddick offered land to the railroad near Millwood Plantation, a large cotton plantation that had been started by Samuel H. Owens about 1853. The land was offered to entice Florida Southern to extend the railroad from McIntosh to Ocala. The settlement called Reddick, started in 1880 and platted two years later, became a general farming center. Stations and later towns that were established along the Florida Southern route through Marion County included McIntosh, Reddick, Lowell, Martin, and Kendrick.

Reddick soon began to prosper as the railroad brought a boom of tourists and new residents to Marion County, and it became an all-important transportation system by which agricultural products were shipped to northern markets. The discovery of lime and phosphate under the soil added new business, as did the growth of the citrus industry around Orange Lake.[1] It was here in Reddick that I was born, a direct descendant of some of the plantation slaves who first cleared and developed the land.

I was the second of six children born to John Albert Thompson (Papa) and Ethel Riley Thompson (Mama). Papa always said he had a small family, and it must have seemed so to him, for his mother had seventeen children.

Mama described my birth this way: It was early in the morning of April 26, 1914. Papa was out on the back porch washing his hands in the only wash basin, made of tin. He had already eaten his breakfast of grits, biscuits, and home-cured bacon.

Mama, as loud as anyone could, called to Papa to hurry and get Aunt Hester, who lived across the sandy dirt road in a framed wood house. Aunt Hester was the midwife for everyone in the neighborhood. She and Uncle Hyman Shandon were not related to us, but because they were older and well respected in the community, everyone called them that. Since their house was right across the road, we could usually just yell to one another from the porch. But this day Mama told Papa to hurry because the baby was coming. Oh, yes, that was the day Idella was brought into the world.

The house where I was born and the farmland surrounding it belonged to my paternal grandfather, Ephraim Ransom, who we called Papa Ephraim. Although he was never married to Papa's mother, he always took care of his children. Besides Papa, he had two daughters, Olive and Idella, for whom I was named. He also helped raise another girl, Lillie, a relative of his wife. He let Papa live in the house, and Papa in turn worked for him on the farm. Papa Ephraim bought and lived in the old Reddick house, the oldest house in Reddick and named for its founder. He was the only black man living in the white neighborhood at the time. He also owned a meat market in Reddick and hired people to work his farmland. He was about five feet seven and 180 pounds, with soft wavy hair. He always dressed neatly, not like a farmer, wearing pants with a belt—never suspenders—and a shirt or sweater. I'm not sure how he came by his wealth, but he was considered the most affluent black man in Reddick at that time.

Ours was a small wood house with a tin roof surrounded by cornfields. It had two wooden doors, one in front and one in the back. There was a living room, an eat-in kitchen, and two bedrooms. The porch along the back of the house had a long bench where we kept the water bucket and a wash basin. Water had to be carried from the neighbor's well or hauled by wagon in a barrel from a pond to our house. As soon as we children were grown enough to draw up the bucket, it was our job to get the water for the next day's use. At Uncle Hyman's deep well the bucket had to be lowered on a rope and then pulled up hand over hand, taking care not to spill it. Well water was used for cooking, drinking, and bathing, primarily. Larger amounts of water were needed for the washing, so we would load the barrel on the wagon drawn by

Top: The house of Idella's grandfather, Papa Ephraim. Also known as the Old Reddick House, it was built about 1895 and is one of the oldest houses in Reddick. Papa Ephraim bought it from Sam Reddick, brother of Reddick's founder, John M. Reddick. Idella's cousin Lil lives in the house today.

Bottom: Papa Ephraim Ransom always dressed neatly, not like a farmer. He owned farmland in Reddick and a meat market in town. He was considered one of the most affluent black men in Reddick at the time.

Papa's horse, George, and go down the road to Uncle Adam Turner's pond. There we scooped up water with the bucket, filling up the barrel, and carried it back to our house.

We also had a cistern near the house that collected rainwater. The house had a few windows with wooden shutters that opened out, but no glass or screens. Mama and Papa slept in one bedroom and the children slept in the other, on two beds. The living room had a large fireplace, and Mama cooked on a tiny wood-burning iron stove in the kitchen. We had a handmade wooden table with a bench on each side, and there were a few straight chairs with wicker bottoms. There were also two rocking chairs, but not much else for furniture.

Our house was not as nice as Aunt Hester's and Uncle Hyman's was, because in those days they were the so-called well-to-do class of blacks. Their house was whitewashed with a kind of paint made of white lime mixed with water, which was used to cover the rough, wide boards around the house. Their house was larger than ours and had four bedrooms. Traveling ministers would stay at their house when they came to Reddick on their circuit.

Aunt Hester and Uncle Hyman owned a farm and had people working for them. They raised cows and chickens and sold milk and eggs to other families. They also had many fruit trees on their property. Uncle Hyman had a two-seat buggy, something our family didn't have. We had to walk almost everywhere we went.

We all loved Aunt Hester. She always wore a long white apron with a big bow tied in back, with long dresses and flat shoes. She would often call us children to her fence and give us cookies or something she knew we did not have. There was no such thing as welfare in those days, but people helped each other out.

My parents were very poor. They seemed to have a hard time trying to take care of the family, and had to move often to find work. When Papa and Mama first married in 1911, they moved to Palmetto, a small town on the west coast of Florida a little south

Uncle Adam Turner's Pond, where the children would go to haul water for the family.

of Tampa, where Papa worked as a box maker (orange crates) for a packinghouse. They lived there until their first child, Hettie, was born in 1913. Then they moved to Reddick and stayed in my grandfather's house, where I was born the following year. Papa had many jobs, but he always farmed and always made boxes wherever he was. The family lived in the little house in Reddick until after my brother, Edward Milton (we called him E. M. for short) was born in 1917.

During the summer and fall of 1918, Papa worked for the railroad. We lived in one of the little houses by the railroad tracks in Reddick during that time. These houses were called section houses and were built for the families of the men who worked as railroad hands. The job involved replacing the railroad ties and keeping the sides of the tracks clean. It was hard work lifting those heavy ties all day long in the summer heat. Both white and black men did this work, and they all lived in the section houses. The men would ride up and down the tracks on a motor car with their tools and lunch pails, repairing track. Papa liked to tell the story of the day the section foreman told them, "Boys, pick up your shovels. The war's over." That was the eleventh day of November 1918.

Mama and her children at the house in Palmetto, 1919. *Left to right, front row:* Idella, age five, E. M., age two, Hettie, age six. *Back row:* Baby Thelma in Mama's arms.

After that, we moved back to Palmetto, where Papa could get work for the winter. My sisters Thelma and Dorothy were born there in 1919 and 1921, respectively. While in Palmetto our family stayed with Papa's cousin, Mary Mitchel. She and her husband had one daughter, Malida, who was older than we children were. Mary's house was not fancy, but it was bigger and better than ours, and it had glass windows. I remember that the house was set high off the ground on stone blocks, and the sandy yard was surrounded by a growth of palmettos and palm trees. It had three bedrooms, two of which were used by Mary's family. The rest of us just slept wherever there was a spot, on pallets of quilts on the floor in the third bedroom or in the living room.

I still recall the day in 1919 when Thelma was born in Mary's house. In those days children weren't told much about childbirth, and Mama and Papa hadn't said anything to us about a baby coming. I just knew Mama had a big belly, but at age five, I had no idea why. Hettie, E. M., and I were sent to play outside, and they wouldn't let us come in for a long time. We must have known something strange was happening as we played under the corner of the house, but it was a complete shock to me when we heard a baby crying. I didn't figure out that Mama's big belly meant a baby was coming until after Eliza, the youngest, was born. Mama never did teach me anything about the "birds and the bees." Anything I did learn came from my more worldly friends. The only thing Mama ever said about the subject (when we were teenagers) was, "Don't you ever come home with no baby." I guess we were just lucky not to, for it was never explained how to avoid it.

When we returned to Reddick we moved in with my mother's father, Papa Jake. His house was built differently than my birth house was. The main part had a big front porch leading into a large living room with a fireplace. There was one bed in the living room, and behind that room were two bedrooms. That part of the house was separated from the kitchen and dining room by an uncovered breezeway. In the breezeway was a long shelf that held the wash basin and water bucket. Two additional bedrooms were built along the breezeway. Papa Jake and his mother, Grandma Nelia, occupied those two rooms, while we stayed in the main part of the house. We were living there when the baby, Eliza, was born in 1923. I especially remember her birth because Papa tried to cook for us while Mama was recuperating. Papa thought he could cook, but I can tell you he couldn't cook like Mama. He fixed liver and white gravy with grits. It tasted terrible, but of course we had to eat it. No, Papa never could cook.

When she was seven years old, my older sister Hettie went to live with Papa's sister, Olive, in Jacksonville. Olive was a school-teacher, and her husband had a good job working for the postal service. They had no children of their own. Olive thought it would help the family out if she took Hettie to live with her and go to school there. Hettie and I, being the two oldest and just a year apart, were very close. We were told in advance that this

Uncle Samuel Smith and Idella's cousin Lillie Mae Ransom, taken in Jacksonville about 1927. Uncle Sam, a mail carrier, was married to Papa's sister, Aunt Olive. They helped raise Idella's sister Hettie and her cousin Lil.

would happen, and we accepted it all right, perhaps not fully understanding—until the day came. Papa drove us in the wagon to the train station in Reddick. Hettie boarded the train holding a paper bag with her sandwich for the trip, and a note with instructions for the conductor. Then we both began to cry, and I cried and waved until the train was out of sight. Hettie later told me that she never did eat that sandwich because she was too upset.

Hettie came home every summer after school was out and spent the summer with us. About two years later, Papa Ephraim sent Lillie to live with Aunt Olive too. Aunt Olive and her husband, Sam, also took in one of Sam's nieces, a girl named Irene. Hettie, consequently, grew up in a bit more affluence than we did. She had a longer school term than we had, she had more clothes and nicer clothes than we did, and she experienced different kinds of store-bought foods and other luxuries that we couldn't afford. It didn't seem to spoil her, however, and it didn't cause any jealousies between us that I can remember. When she was grown, Hettie always remembered to help out Mama and Papa.

Both Mama and Papa worked in the fields, and as soon as I was old enough, about seven or eight years old, I was expected to help take care of the younger children. So with the help of my brother, E. M., I became the second mama to my younger sisters, babysitting them while Mama and Papa worked. There were always peanuts to shell, and plenty of other chores to keep us busy. Every day we were each given a quota of peanuts to get shelled. Big farmers in the area paid people to shell their peanuts, which were sold for seed. All the poor people did this as a way to make extra money, and in our family, we all helped. So we would sit on the steps, shelling our quota of three or four quarts, and put them in bushel burlap bags. Then we would have to clean up all the peanut hulls and pile them in the hog pen for the hogs to eat. Nothing was ever thrown away or wasted back then.

Left to right: Papa Jake (Idella's maternal grandfather), Idella, and Eliza in front of Hettie's house in Jacksonville in 1944.

I remember one time I was caring for the children when Eliza was still a baby. E. M. and I wanted to go play in the cornfields with the neighbor children and pick some wild blackberries. We thought of a way to keep Eliza still so we wouldn't have to carry her with us. We dug a hole in the sand and started to cover up her legs so she couldn't crawl away. We had sand covering her all the way up to her arms when a neighbor woman passed by and saw what we were up to.

"Get that baby outta that sand!" she hollered.

Of course, she went straight to tell Mama, and you know what happened next. Mama wore us out, all the while telling us, "You could have smothered her to death!" We were duly scared, and needless to say we didn't go anywhere to play that day.

During the late fall and winter, after the growing season was over at home, Papa often went south to Fort Myers or Miami to find work. Most times he went alone and was gone two or three months. He worked several jobs, in restaurants waiting tables, cutting meat as a butcher, and always making boxes. Papa was one of Marion County's best box makers, and he made boxes for all the big orange grove dealers. He always came home in time for spring planting and watermelon season. Papa farmed for himself for a long time, and later began to sharecrop, becoming one of the main sharecroppers with big farmers in the area. His largest crop was watermelon, but he also grew a lot of okra, beans, peas, and corn.

I'll never forget the winter Mama decided to go with Papa to get a job for that season, leaving us children with Papa Jake. I must have been about thirteen years old. Papa went first in the fall of the year and then sent for Mama once he got a job and was settled. Mama intended to go by herself, but just as she was leaving, Thelma started hollering, so that Mama threw some things in a bag for her and took her with her. Looking back, although I'm sure it wouldn't have done any good, I wished I'd have hollered too. The rest of us—E. M., Dorothy, Eliza, and I—stayed in the house with Papa Jake and his mother, Grandma Nelia, who had been living with him for some time. I was the one left with Mama's work to do, for Grandma Nelia was senile and no help at all. I had to fix Papa Jake's dinner bucket, and do the washing, ironing, cooking, and babysitting.

Papa Jake was not married, for his wife had died some years before. One morning as he left for work, he told me to wash his socks because he was going out that evening. He must have owned just the one pair of dress socks, and I forgot to wash them during the day. When I saw him coming, I suddenly remembered the socks. I was scared, and in my panic, without thinking it through, I ran and rinsed them out real quick. Of course, there was no way to get them dry in time. Papa Jake took a bath, got dressed, and then called for his socks. When he discovered they were wringing wet, he was furious. He beat me hard with his leather strap. I was indignant. How could Mama have left us like that? It just wasn't fair. When she got back I told her about it, and I guess she was sorry because she didn't ever leave us again.

As far as I can remember, Papa—hard as he worked—never complained about being tired. When we children would complain about being tired, he would say, "Do you know, children, that there are people in this world who never work, sit all day long, and they complain saying, 'I am so tired'? At least you can see some results of your being tired, so let's work."

Mama did not go out to work often, except to help Papa in the fields, but she worked plenty hard at home. She was always up early in the kitchen fixing food buckets and seeing that all the chores were done before we left for school. She was a good house-keeper and the best cook in town. Our meals were simple, fash-

Hog-killing was a big annual event for Idella's family. Several neighbors came to help. The men would cut up the meat while the women made sausage and chitterlings. The children's job was to keep the fires going. At the end of the day everyone would stop to eat a meal prepared by the women.

ioned mainly with food we were able to raise on our farm. We always had a vegetable garden, and grew almost every kind of vegetable you can think of.

Papa raised hogs kept in a pen, and once a year we had a hog killing. Three or four neighbors would gather at our house and help with the butchering. The hog was usually killed by shooting it in the head, or sometimes it was hit with a hammer. The men would cut up the meat while the women cleaned off the head and used the scraps to make sausage and head cheese. Sausage was ground, seasoned and stuffed into clean intestine casings. Any extra intestines were made into chitterlings. Lard was made from the fat and used in cooking and in making lye soap. Some meat was carried to the meatpacking house in Fairfield to be cured, and then it was hung in our smokehouse. Every home had a smokehouse where meat was stored. Nothing was ever wasted. The children's job was to keep the fires going. Along about three or four o'clock in the afternoon the women would have the scraps cooked for dinner and everyone would stop to eat.

When we lived with Papa Jake we also had cows, white-faced Herefords, as I recall. We kept enough cows to provide us with milk, plus one to butcher each year and some to sell. We also raised chickens that were kept in a chicken coop. That was the one job I despised, having to go in that stinky chicken coop, slimy with droppings, and collect eggs or feed the hens.

Some of Papa's corn crop was ground at the mill each year and made into grits and corn meal. These were the staples of our diet. Flour had to be bought and so was used sparingly, and sweets made with store-bought sugar were only for special occasions. Papa raised sugar cane, from which we made cane syrup. This was our main sweetener. We often drank what we called "sweet'n water" with our dinner. Just as its name implies, it was made simply by stirring a little cane syrup into a glass of water. Mama also made a drink she called "everlasting tea." It was made from a weed we gathered in the woods. I don't remember its name or if I ever knew its name, but it was a grayish-colored sort of grass with a fuzzy white flower. The plant was dried and the stems and leaves were boiled to make the tea.

Potatoes grown in Papa's garden became another food staple for our family. Mama even used them to make a dessert we called "potato pound," a cake-like pudding made in a mold. Sweet potato pie was another favorite treat, especially at Thanksgiving and Christmas. Gingerbread, made with cane syrup instead of sugar, was often served as a Sunday dessert. Mama frequently made teacakes for our dessert. These were sweet biscuits, rolled and cut out with a glass and baked in the oven. For a special treat, Mama would send us children out to the fields to pick blackberries or blueberries, and she would make a sort of cobbler by cooking them on top of the stove with sugar and adding dumplings.

How we looked forward to holidays, particularly Thanksgiving and Christmas! That was the only time Mama made things like chocolate cake, and she always baked four or five cakes and pies. All the family got together for these occasions. Poor as we were, Mama and Papa always made Christmas a special time for us children. On Christmas Eve we would each hang our stocking, the biggest sock we could find, on nails around the fireplace. We firmly believed that it was Santa Claus who came down the chimney and filled the stockings that night. On Christmas morning we would delight in such treasures as a few pieces of candy, some nuts, a new pair of socks or a ribbon, maybe a pencil or pad of paper, and always one apple and a stick of peppermint. I was nine or ten years old before I knew it wasn't Santa who had put those gifts in my stocking. That year, Mama took me with her to Dupree's store when she was buying the presents, although I didn't know what she was doing at the time. As we were admiring all the little trinkets, she held up a pretty glass bowl and asked me, "Sister, you like this?" I didn't see her buy it, but when it appeared in my stocking on Christmas morning I knew the truth.

When we were a little older, we were allowed to stay up until midnight on New Year's Eve. Usually we would go to a special church service. Deacons would watch the time, and at midnight the church bells would ring in the new year.

Another favorite childhood event was the Marion County Fair. My aunt Idella, Papa's sister, was the first black homemaking teacher working for the Extension Service. I took cooking and sewing classes held at our school on Friday evenings, and would enter sewing or cooking projects in the fair. Aunt Idella had a car and would take us to the fair. There we had a grand time riding the rides and hollering with mock fear and glee.

Whenever we were sick with colds and such, Mama's remedy was always a dose of castor oil. How we hated that stuff! Lillie told me that Papa Ephraim's wife used to give her nine drops of turpentine on a teaspoon of sugar to cure most anything. I don't remember Mama giving us anything like that, and thinking about it, I guess the castor oil wasn't so bad.

Each day, it seemed, Mama had to wash, making sure we all had a clean change of clothes. There was no washing machine; Mama only had a washboard and pot. Washing clothes was a long job. First Mama would sort the clothes by colors, much as one does today. That's where the similarity to today's washing ends, however. Washing was done outdoors. Mama had a long bench on which she put three washtubs filled with water. Soap powder, which we called gold dust powder, was added to the first tub. Each piece of clothing was scrubbed on the washboard and rubbed until it was clean in this tub. Then it was wrung out and placed in the first rinse water, wrung out again and placed in the second rinse tub. Then the load was put in the boil pot with more soap. The boil pot was a large, black cast-iron pot filled with water and set up on bricks or stones. A fire was built under the pot, and the water was heated until it was boiling. Mama would use a longhandled wooden paddle to keep pushing the clothes down in the boil pot. The clothes were boiled for about twenty or thirty minutes. While they were in the boil pot, the rinse tubs had to be emptied and fresh water put in them. Mama would dip the clothes in and out of the boiling water with the stick and then put them in a drain pot. The drain pot was carried to the coldwater rinse tubs, where the clothes were put through two more rinses. Clothes were then wrung out and hung piece by piece on wire lines to dry. We had four clotheslines, each about sixty feet long.

The next day was the ironing. Mama heated the iron on top of the wood stove. A homemade ironing board, covered with old sheets or blankets for padding, rested across two straight chairs placed back to back. Everything had to be ironed, and much of it starched as well. Mama mixed Argo starch in a bowl with water. Parts to be starched, such as collars and cuffs, were dipped in the bowl of liquid starch and left to dry before being ironed. Finally everything had to be folded neatly and put away. We had long open shelves in our bedroom where folded clothes were placed.

Mama made most of our clothes, and also sewed for many people in the community. This brought in a little extra money. During the day, especially in the winter while the children were at school, Mama and one or two other ladies would quilt. They made some lovely quilts for each family.

Mama said from the beginning that I was an unusual child. She meant, I guess, that I was different from my brother and sisters because I rarely complained about having to do my share. Mama said she never had to tell me what to do; I was always willing to help her in the kitchen, doing the washing and ironing, and looking after the younger children. I was taught to work, but I also enjoyed it and took pride in it.

CHAPTER 2

School Days

EVEN THOUGH Papa never completed school, he meant for all of his children to have an education. Once we started school, we never missed a day unless we were sick, except for the winters we spent in Palmetto. We all studied and learned because our parents took the time to help each one of us.

In those days, long before integration, there were no public schools for blacks. Informal schools were held in private homes with untrained teachers. There was no set age to send children to school, and so I began my education in this way when I was about four years old.

The house where we went to school was about two miles away. A teenage neighbor girl, Annie Ray Taylor (Uncle Adam's grand-daughter), would pick us up and walk with us along the sandy road from our house and by shortcut trails through the woods. We would climb the stairs of the two-story house to the room where we had school. It was not set up like a classroom, with desks and such. I remember kneeling at a sort of bench to color or scratch on my paper. We had to be very careful with our paper, for we were only allotted one or two sheets a day. There was just one teacher who taught us all, about fifteen to twenty students of all different ages. I can't remember who that first teacher was or any details about her.

The school term for blacks was only three months long in the winter. The rest of the year, children were needed to help at home or in the fields, tending crops. School was only for spare time between crops. Mama made us dresses for school, and we had one Sunday dress. We each had a sweater and one pair of shoes and socks, which had to last. We were taught to take care of our things, for there was no money to go out and buy new things if we didn't. Someone, a neighbor or friend, always gave us a coat that had been outgrown by their children, for it was cold walking to school in the winter.

Before we set off for school, there were chores to do. Papa got us up at 4:30 or 5:00 every morning to feed the hogs and the chickens, gather eggs, feed and milk the cows, carry water, and gather wood. Mama reminded us not to forget to get up enough wood chips for the clothes pot, for it seemed almost every day she had to wash. The chores were divided among the children as we got big enough. We did them and were never late to school.

Mama fixed us each a lunch bucket, a tin pail about pint-size with our name on it. In it she would put a biscuit sandwich— either white potato, which Papa grew, or bacon from the hogs we raised. Sometimes we had Mama's homemade jelly on our biscuit. Mama made us teacakes or sweetbread for dessert. We drank water from the school.

After school we had to hurry home, for there were more chores to do around the house. We had to go into the woods and gather dead limbs and cut them for the woodpile on the porch. Wood was needed every day for the fireplace and the stove. We had to keep that woodpile full. Every evening we would sit around the kerosene lamp, our only light, and do our studies. Mama always checked our papers before we went to bed.

The first year in school was called the ABC class, because that's what we learned. From there we got our first book, the primer. The two-story wood house on the north side of Reddick was soon destroyed by fire. I was too young to understand, and I don't recall the reason the house burned. I just remember that when we got up that day, they said the school was burning. After that happened, we attended school in one of three churches: Mount Cello, Mount Olive Baptist, or Mount Zion Methodist. All of these churches were in a row, not far apart, on the dirt road we called Church Street, although Mount Cello was a little farther away, on the other side of Dixie Highway. The churches took turns hosting the school. Later, the school was moved to the Masonic Hall, near our church, where they let us have a down-stairs room.

Each morning the students would have to line up by grades outside the door, and when the teacher rang the bell we would walk inside single file and take our seats. The teacher called the roll, and we would have to holler "Present," when she called our name. Next we said the pledge of allegiance, and then we had devotion. During devotion students would recite Bible verses they had memorized. Each of us had verses to learn, and I remember Mama always helped us practice ours. We would sing a song, usually a hymn or spiritual. I couldn't sing well, but other children loved to lead the class in song. Some of them had beautiful voices and were often chosen as song leader. Devotion time always ended with a prayer.

We were taught reading, spelling, arithmetic, history, and geography, but not all subjects were taught every day. I remember history was always taught near the end of the week and other subjects on different days.

The teacher appointed a parliamentarian to help her keep order in the classroom. That person's job was to take down the names of those who did something wrong. Offenses included talking or laughing out loud, moving around the room without permission, throwing paper, or sticking someone with your pencil. We never knew until the end of the day who the parliamentarian was, for that was when the teacher called for the report. The teacher would punish the offenders by spanking them with a long wooden paddle in front of everybody. It happened to me many times, because my mouth always got me in trouble. I could always be caught talking, laughing or whispering. Even though the parliamentarian was not very popular with the other students, when it was my turn to be the parliamentarian, I was happy to do it. It was my chance to get back at those who caused me to be punished.

We did not have to attend school in the Masonic Hall building very long, for when I was in about the seventh grade, we had a "real" school building. Financed in part by a program known as the Rosenwald Fund, Mount Zion Elementary, as it was called, became the first public school for blacks in Reddick. Hoping to improve the lives of former slaves, Northern mission groups and philanthropists helped fund many schools for blacks in the early years of the century.

The Rosenwald Fund was named for its founder, Julius Rosenwald, a Jewish businessman who was president of Sears, Roebuck & Company of Chicago. He established the fund in 1917 in response to a request by the prominent black educator, Booker T. Washington, for help in building schools for blacks throughout the rural South. Applicants for assistance had to agree to certain building specifications and to provide local funds from both private donations and county taxes.[1] In accordance with the agreement, black citizens of Reddick raised money to help buy the land where the school was to be constructed. The Marion County school board provided $504.80 to purchase materials, and the Rosenwald Fund gave $900 to have the building sealed, painted, and finished.[2] Completed by contractor B. F. Mims in February of 1926, the new Mount Zion Elementary was built under the shade of oak trees near Highway 25A. The large wooden building had four classrooms, two on each side, with a long hallway between. There were closets for our coats and lunch pails, and glass windows. There was a principal who was the head teacher, and three other teachers who taught grades one through eight. I remember my first teacher, Miss Etta Ward, and later I had Mrs. Street. The county hired all the teachers for this school.

Papa and Mama had to buy our school supplies, which consisted of a tablet, which was our composition book; one pencil; and our primer or textbook. The books were passed down from one child to the next, so we were taught to keep up with and take care of our book.

I had three good friends during my years at Mount Zion. They were Mamie Rogers, Annie May Jenkins, and Addie Bell Monroe. Every day at our lunch recess we would sit outside on the ground under the oak trees to share our lunches and talk. I still remember the time Addie Bell hit me in my head when we were playing basketball in the schoolyard. I didn't shoot and make the basket that she thought I should have. I don't know how in the world she got up to me so fast, but just as I missed she reached over and knocked me in the head. (We still tease about it today.) About the only time I had to socialize with friends was at school. Mama and Papa never let us bring friends home to play. They were very strict, and we had our chores to do. Sometimes Papa would pick us up at school to go work on the farm, picking peanuts or okra, before we went home to do our other chores.

Throughout these early years, my education would be interrupted each time we moved to Palmetto for the winter. We never attended school in Palmetto, but Mama and Papa would teach us reading, spelling and counting during those times. And we always moved back to Reddick when we could.

There were ten of us in the eighth grade class at Mount Zion in 1927. From there some students went on to high school, while many others quit school to go to work or to get married. My friend Mamie Rogers went on to high school and became a teacher. She taught in Leesburg for a while. When the war broke out she married a fellow who was in the service, and they moved to Jacksonville, where her husband was stationed at Cecil Field. I was visiting Hettie in Jacksonville when Mamie got sick and passed. To keep Mamie in my mind forever, I named one of my godsons Lawrence, after Mamie's married name. Annie May Jenkins continued to live in Reddick, but she didn't go on to school. She had a baby girl. It was just about six years ago now that she was moved to a nursing home in Ocala, where she still lives. Addie Bell also did not go on to school after eighth grade. Today she lives in Jacksonville and has two children.

The next year after completing the eighth grade at Mount Zion, I attended part of a term at Fessenden Academy. Fessenden was the high school for blacks in the area, located about eight miles south of Reddick in a settlement called Martin. Started in a log cabin in 1868, Union School, as it was called, was one of the schools financed by mission groups from the North who wanted to improve the lives of former slave families.[3] The school was renamed Fessenden Academy in honor of Ferdinand Stone Fessenden, who was instrumental in having a larger, better-equipped facility built in 1890.[4] It was a boarding school, as children had no way to travel back and forth to home every day. Mama and Papa had to pay twenty-five cents a month for me to go there, and I had to work in the kitchen and laundry to pay for my board. It was my first time being away from home. The school term was a little longer than before, about four months instead of three. Yet I didn't have time to get homesick, for we were kept busy. The bell

Unidentified girl walking in front of Fessenden Academy near the community of Martin, Florida, where Idella attended ninth grade.

would ring in the morning and we would all go to breakfast. The day was then filled with classes and work. After work was study time and then lights out.

Mama took me out of Fessenden before I finished the ninth grade and sent me to Bethune-Cookman Institute in Daytona Beach. That was in 1928. I'm not exactly sure why Mama did this, but it may be that Bethune-Cookman had a better reputation for those who were interested in a good education. Mary McLeod Bethune started the school for black girls and united it with Cookman Institute of Jacksonville in 1923. Bethune-Cookman Institute was open to both boys and girls.[5] Other girls from the Reddick area went there, and Mama's friend, Martha Crawford, whose daughter attended school there, may have influenced Mama to send me as well.

Bethune-Cookman was also a boarding school for black students. Mama and Papa had to pay two or three dollars a semester for me to attend. The Bethune-Cookman campus had one boys' and one girls' dormitory, each with a dorm mother in charge. There was a gymnasium, a cafeteria, and an infirmary. The two-story classroom building was between the gym and the infirmary. In the girls' dormitory, where I lived, each room had two beds. My first roommate was Benney Kinsler. She and I remained friends for all of our adult lives. Benney became a schoolteacher and taught for fifty-eight years in Mount Dora. There were strict rules and curfews to be followed, but we all loved Mrs. Bethune. She knew all the students by name, and she would come out on the campus in the afternoon and talk to us under the shade of the trees. She would teach us how to be ladies during these sessions. She would tell us how to sit and walk, how to cross our legs at the ankles and not at the knees.

Idella attended the Bethune-Cookman Institute in Daytona Beach from 1928 to 1929. Mary McLeod Bethune taught the girls how to be ladies. On Sunday morning the girls would dress in their uniforms and sing as Mrs. Bethune led them in line to the auditorium for church services. Photo courtesy of Florida State Archives.

The students wore uniforms of white blouses and blue skirts. The athletic uniform consisted of white blouses and wide-legged bloomers that had elastic at the knees. Curfew was at eight o'clock, the time we all had to be in our dorms. We had study period until nine o'clock, when all lights had to be out. On Sunday there would be morning church service in the auditorium, Bible study, and concerts or "sings." I remember we would all sing as we lined up and walked to the auditorium on Sunday morning.

I finished two winter terms at Bethune-Cookman, but I was suffering from an ulcerated stomach and gallstones and had to return home.

Dr. Strange from McIntosh came to the house and treated me for my illness, but I had to miss a term of school. When I was well and Mama wanted to send me back, I refused to go. I would be behind all of my friends, I said, and all my classmates would be younger than I would. That was when Mama's friend, Mrs. Crawford, encouraged me to take the Florida State Teachers' Exam, given in Gainesville.

I had known Mrs. Martha Crawford all my life. Besides being a friend of Mama's, she was one of Reddick's first black educators. She had been principal and head teacher when we had school in the churches and at the Masonic Hall. I remember her for the kindness and concern she showed to everyone. Mrs. Martha, as we affectionately called her, always had the children at school share her lunch with her. I can hear her now, saying—whenever we would go to her with a problem—"Now wait. Take your time and tell me what happened."

Mrs. Martha was very sincere and felt strongly about letting Christianity guide her lifestyle. She had great respect for the law and for those in authority, and she felt great love toward mankind, regardless of color. She refused to ridicule or to speak maliciously about people at any time. You could not talk about unbecoming things around Mrs. Martha Crawford.

Mrs. Martha believed that education was something due everyone. She said that as long as an individual lives and has a craving to learn and explore, let him do so, regardless of age. She always told us to wear out our minds and not let them rust out. She would go out of her way to do a favor for anyone. She always had encouraging words to give the struggling—young and old alike— who were trying to reach higher. She did not believe in compromising and settling for anything less than one's best. And so it was that Mrs. Martha would not allow me to give up on education, and she encouraged me to become a teacher.

In 1929, you did not have to attend college or even finish high school to become a teacher. If you were smart enough to answer the questions and pass the teacher's exam, you could teach. So I went to Gainesville and took the exam. I passed and was awarded a certificate to teach in the black schools in Florida. For each of the next three summers, I returned to Bethune-Cookman for summer school in order to extend my teaching certificate.

My first teaching job was in the winter of 1929 at a school in Gulf Hammock, located west of Reddick in Levy County. I was fifteen years old. The school served blacks in first through eighth grade. There were two teachers, but we both taught in the same big room. I taught the beginners through fourth grade, and the other teacher taught the older students. I was young and not too sure of myself, and the children seemed to be almost as big as I was. The other teacher helped me out a lot, showing me what to do.

I lived with my aunt Gertrude, one of Papa's sisters who was a teacher too, at another school. A hammock is a forested area of land above the level of a marsh, so as its name implies, Gulf Hammock was in the woods. There were no paved streets there, just narrow sandy trails to the store and to the schools. Aunt Gertrude's and Uncle Nathan's little wood house was in a thick area of forest, with no other houses near it. I taught "uptown" in the so-called big school. I guess we called it that because we had two teachers instead of one. Aunt Gertrude taught at a tiny place on the other side of Gulf Hammock, where it was too far for children to walk to the big school. She was the only teacher there.

I paid Aunt Gertrude about five dollars a month for my room and board. At the end of each month I would receive my check for thirty dollars, which I considered a lot of money in those days. I would catch a ride home to Reddick by sharing gas money with someone. On the way home we would stop at the food store in Williston, where I would cash my check and buy a bag of groceries to take home to Mama. Each month I would give Mama ten or fifteen dollars from my check to help out the family. I used the remainder for my expenses, and once in a while I would buy myself some new clothes.

Except for church on Sundays, there was no social life for me in Gulf Hammock. My days were filled with school, preparing lessons, and doing laundry. There would be a little while to eat and talk, and then I'd go to bed.

It was in Gulf Hammock that I first learned to shoot a gun. Uncle Nathan was a great hunter. He was half Indian, so I believe it was in his blood to be out in the woods and hunt. When we had time, Uncle Nathan had me practice shooting at tin cans. He gave me a rifle—not a double-barrel shotgun—and taught me to shoot, and I just kept it with me all the time. Everywhere I would go after that, I would take my gun, including to Cross Creek.

After the three-month school term, I returned home to work in the fields during the spring and summer. I made ninety dollars, or thirty dollars a month, that first three-month term. White teachers like Virginia Cromartie, the daughter of the local judge, was also a beginning teacher that year and made forty dollars a month.

It wasn't hard to find a teaching job in those days, for there weren't many blacks who were qualified. Aunt Gertrude had heard about the opening in Gulf Hammock, and told me to go to the superintendent's office to sign up for the job. Transportation was a big problem that first year, always having to pay someone to take me home, so Mrs. Martha Crawford got me a job closer to home the next school term, the winter of 1930.

That job was in Marion County, teaching in a small wooden building on Highway 316 near Sparr. Poor black students attended there from their homes in the woods of East Reddick and Sparr. It was called Jacob's Well School. There were about fifteen farmers' children altogether, and I was the only teacher there. It was about a three-mile walk from my house, for I stayed at home that year. That's when I bought my first car, a used four-door blue Chevy. It cost $150. Papa Ephraim gave me fifty dollars towards it, and I paid the rest on time. I already knew how to drive, for Papa had taught me to drive the truck around the fields when I was about twelve years old. In those days nobody was required to have a driver's license, just as there were no posted speed limits. We just drove.

I remember once E. M. and I "borrowed" Papa's truck to go about two miles up to some friends' houses. I drove, and on the way back the truck stopped. Well, there wasn't any gas in it. I could drive, but I didn't know anything about the gas gauge on the truck, so I didn't think about running out of gas. We had to walk home, leaving Papa's truck up the road. So Papa found out we'd been taking his truck without telling him. He didn't whip me; he just scolded me, telling me to always ask before using anybody's things. Then he had to walk up to the Reddick station to get some gas in a can and carry it back up to where the truck was. He said, "Now don't you ever do that again. You ask me first."

Anyway, I drove my blue Chevy to and from work at Jacob's Well School, but I didn't get to keep it for long.

The following year, in 1931, I was hired by what was then Polk County to teach in the black community of Wauchula. Papa kept my car, and I never did get it back. I rode the train to Lakeland, where I was met by the supervisor of the black school. He took me first to the courthouse to fill out the necessary papers, then we had to drive about ten miles down the road to "black town," as it was called. I stayed there in a rooming house. One night during that term, I went to a dance in town. The supervisor, who was not an educator himself, was there and informed me that teachers were not allowed to attend dances. That's when I decided that I wouldn't go back after the term, and that teaching was not what Idella wanted for a lifetime career. If I couldn't dance or socialize as young as I was, then I would look for something else besides teaching.

I convinced my mother that I could find a better job if I could go to West Palm Beach, where I could live with Mrs. Rosa Heath, a friend of the family. This was agreed to, and I was happy to leave Reddick and begin a new life in the city.

During the winters of 1932 and 1933, I shared a room with Miss Rosa and did laundry for rich people vacationing in Palm Beach. The housing accommodations were not much to my liking, although I did meet many types of people while living there. The house we stayed in was on the corner of Sapodilla Avenue and Eighth Street. It was a busy street corner, with a taxi stand and a fruit stand, which were run by Rosa's brother. People stopped and talked there day and night, some dressed up in fancy clothes. This was all new to me, and I was excited by it. I made many friends and found a big Baptist church that I started attending on Sundays. Tabernacle Missionary Baptist had one of the largest black congregations in West Palm Beach, I found out. After the first month of attending, I knew that if I was going to join this church I would have to buy some new dresses. These people certainly did wear some fine-looking clothes. Of course, I was not able to buy any clothes and pay for my board too, so I had to think of another way.

One night after I had united with the church, I went to the church choir meeting and told the president I would like to join the choir. Oh, he was happy to have a new member join, but what he didn't know was that I could not sing. The members of the choir had to wear robes, you see, and so that solved my clothing problem. I was placed on the second row of this big choir (perhaps because of my awful voice), and I wore my robe to church proudly every Sunday.

West Palm Beach was very different from Reddick and other places in Marion County. There were theaters just for blacks, so we did not have to go to the "attic," as we called the balconies where blacks had to sit in the theater in Ocala. I was invited to nice restaurants and nightclubs. There were lovely parks and shuffleboard games. There was always something to do as soon as I came in from work. Oh, how happy I was, for West Palm Beach offered many exciting times.

After two winters doing laundry with Rosa, I found a nice job working for the Bowens, a lovely couple who lived on Florida Avenue. Mr. J. O. Bowen was the manager of Southern Dairies Ice Cream Company in Miami. In the Bowens' home I learned correct table setting, and how to cook all types of fancy foods. Mama was a good country cook, but here I learned how to prepare and serve luncheons and big dinner parties.

Figuring myself grown, I rented my own room, no longer sharing a room with Rosa. I worked for the Bowens for five years, from 1934 until after Christmas in 1939. I probably would have continued working for them except for a romance gone bad. Life in West Palm Beach was so different from the country life I was used to, and I thought at the time I would live there forever. I was swept off my feet by a sophisticated charmer from Nassau, the Bahamas, a fancy dresser and smooth talker. I was in love and yet I knew I was doing wrong. This boyfriend and I had a major misunderstanding and I felt threatened. I had to get away from him, somewhere that this city man would dare not come. I decided it was time for me to return to Reddick and to forget the city life.

As I mentioned earlier, Papa saw to it that all of his children were educated. I remember once when it was time for Florida Normal College (now called Florida Memorial College) to open, Eliza was slow about deciding to go back for her last year. As he was washing his hands, Papa said, "Liz, it seems you can't make up your mind about finishing college, so I am going to make it up for you. Get in there and get your things together, for we will be going over [to St. Augustine] first thing in the morning." Well, this was done, and not another word did Papa have to say, for we were taught to obey.

All of my sisters finished school and went on to careers in teaching or nursing, the only two choices for blacks in those days. Hettie completed training at Brewster Hospital as a nurse, and was given a job there as a teacher of nurses. Once we were working, Hettie and I both helped Mama and Papa put the other children through school. Mama always said to us, "If anyone ever needs anything, you share." That's what was expected back then, and that's what we did. I'm sure a lot of families wouldn't have made it otherwise. Thelma and Eliza finished college at Florida Normal College in St. Augustine. They both taught in Florida public schools until they retired. Thelma went down to Pompano Beach in Broward County to teach. She made more money there than teachers did in Marion County. Dorothy graduated from

Papa and "his girls," 1984.

Idella's brother, Edward Milton Thompson (E. M.), in uniform in 1943.

Sadie Thompson, about 1969. E. M. married Sadie while he was home on his first furlough during World War II. He was overseas when their baby, Joyce Ann, was born, and was killed in action before he ever saw her.

nursing school at Brewster Hospital and worked for the Marion County Medical Center for thirty-one years before retiring.

Meanwhile my brother E. M. finished school at Florida Normal College, and he worked and practiced embalming at Delia Brown's Funeral Home in Ocala. He was hoping to attend a mortician school in upper New York State, but was called to duty in the service before he had the chance. On his first furlough he married Sadie Jenkins, and soon a child was on the way. His baby girl was born in 1944 while he was away at war. He sent his wife the name Joyce Ann, but tragically he was killed in action and never got to see his daughter.

My formal education did not end when I quit teaching. During the time I was working for Mrs. Rawlings (which was to come soon), I attended beauty school. She sent me partly because I told her I would like to, and partly so I could learn to do her hair for her. I started at Apex Beauty School in Atlanta, Georgia, and completed the course at Angelo Beauty School in Tampa, Florida. This education helped me to earn a living after I left Mrs. Rawlings.

I would also eventually return to teaching, and when I did, I took courses at Miami-Dade Community College to renew my teaching certificate.

In addition to teaching school, I also taught Sunday school for many years. I taught an adult Sunday school class in Fort Lauderdale for three years under the direction of Reverend Weaver and the Sunday school superintendent, Deacon Williams. In 1986, after moving to Ocala to help care for Papa when he took sick, I united with the New Zion Missionary Baptist Church. At the time there was just one adult Sunday school class.

Early in 1987, Reverend E. F. Broxton paid me a visit at my house. He came to ask me if I would help organize another adult Sunday school class. He talked about other Sunday school teach-

Above: Idella's church in Ocala, New Zion Missionary Baptist Church. At Reverend Broxton's urging, Idella was instrumental in expanding the adult Sunday-school classes at the church.

Left: Idella's pastor, Reverend E. F. Broxton.

ers he had worked with and the degrees they had. I said to him, "Rev, I have one degree."

"You have a degree?" he asked.

"Yes, it's a D.T.T."

"What kind of degree is that?" he wanted to know.

"It's a degree in talking, teaching, and serving others given to me by Jesus Christ," I told him. So it was agreed that I would take the new class. There wasn't much spare room in the church, so at first the class was taught in the kitchen. Word got around that I was teaching a class, and before we knew it we had twenty-eight new members in my Sunday school class. They had to move us from the kitchen to the choir stand. Today, in 1999, the church has five adult Sunday school classes.

Aside from my formal schooling, I have discovered that every day there is the opportunity to learn something. Most of our education comes from our experiences, and I have had a lot of those. When it comes to life's school, I am a very educated person.

CHAPTER 3 »

Hand-Me-Down Stories

WE HAVE NO written record to prove it, but all our lives we were told that our family was descended from the line of the well-known slave Nat Turner. He was the leader of a black slave revolt, later known as Turner's Rebellion, against the white plantation owners in Virginia in 1831. He was responsible for the largest massacre of slave owners in the United States.

Papa told us that Henderson Turner, Nat Turner's brother, was the father of Will and Adam Turner, who were brought to Marion County, Florida, as slaves. Will Turner was Papa's grandfather. His daughter, Vinie, was Papa's mother.

Grandma Vinie's farm was located on State Road 316, east of Uncle Adam's pond. As children we loved to travel along the paths through the fields to visit Grandma Vinie. While most of her seventeen children were grown, her baby boy, my uncle Walter, was the same age as I was. Grandma Vinie was a good cook, and she always gave us something when we visited her,

Grandma Vinie (Idella's paternal grandmother) on the right, with her sister, Lizzie (Mary Mitchel's mother-in-law from Palmetto). Grandma Vinie had seventeen children, and Papa was the oldest.

white beans or one of her big fat biscuits. Mama would send us over there but would always tell us, "Now, don't you go beg Miss Vinie to eat while you're there."

We also loved to visit Uncle Adam, who was in his nineties and still living on his farm near Grandma Vinie's. Uncle Adam lived in an old log cabin with a rock chimney, two wooden windows and a door that opened from the outside. Rocks on each side of the doorway were used to hold up a piece of board that formed the step leading up to the front room. The cabin had two rooms, with beds in each one, and a stove and wooden table in the front room, where the fireplace was. Uncle Adam's daughter, Mary Taylor, and a granddaughter, Annie Ray Taylor, lived with him. Uncle Adam slept in the front room. There was always plenty of wood in the corner, and it seemed to me that each time we went to see Uncle Adam there was a fire going in the fireplace.

Uncle Adam was a short man, not more than five feet tall. His salt-and-pepper hair was bushy and unkempt. He also had a long beard and mustache that together with his hair made him rather wild looking, something that both frightened and delighted us children. He always wore overalls with straps that crossed in the back, and if it was cold he wore a checkered flannel shirt underneath. I never did see him with shoes on; he was always barefoot. Uncle Adam was famous for telling weird stories. I believe he must have made up most of the stories he told, many of which were scary stories about bears and other creatures in the woods. He had a ferocious voice that could send shivers down my back, and he talked about eating children.

I'm not sure why I kept going back to his house. I guess the stories he told were as interesting as they were terrifying. I was especially fascinated when he told true stories about his own life. He would sit in his chair by the fire, smoking his pipe as he spoke, and he liked us children to comb his hair. So we would stand around him and run a comb through his tangled, woolly hair as we listened to him recount the stories of his past.

He told us how his family was brought over on a slave ship, and how they were sold and divided from their families. He told us about Nat Turner, who was left back in Virginia when they were sent to live in this woody country place that was later named Reddick. Uncle Adam said, "Never did I see him again."

We know what happened to Nat Turner, by the historical accounts and by his own recorded confessions. Nat Turner was born in 1800, the son of Nancy Turner. His mother had been taken from Africa while in her teens and sold to Benjamin Turner, a Virginia plantation owner. She was given the name Nancy and the surname of her master. The identity of Nat's father isn't known, except that he was a second-generation slave. As a child Nat's mother taught him about his African heritage. She told him that certain marks on his skin were spiritual signs that he would one day become a prophet. Nat was taught to read and write along with his master's son Samuel; and his grandmother, Bridget, who had been converted, taught him Christianity. In 1810 Benjamin Turner died, leaving his slaves to his son Samuel. In 1828 Nat was sold to Thomas Moore, then sold again to Putnam Moore, who loaned him to a relative, Joseph Travis. All of the owners lived close together, so Nat was able to maintain contact with some of his family and friends. He became a popular religious leader among his fellow slaves and believed that he had been chosen by God to lead his people to freedom.[1]

Following a solar eclipse that he believed was a sign from heaven, Nat made plans to begin a revolt. On August 21, 1831, he and five other slaves killed Joseph Travis and his family, then proceeded to kill Samuel Turner and his family as well. Later joined by about sixty blacks from neighboring plantations, the group started a general revolt, ultimately killing more than fifty whites. White militiamen squashed the rebellion within a few days, and many blacks were lynched in revenge by white mobs. Turner himself was captured about six weeks later and was eventually tried and hanged. After Turner's Rebellion, slaves began a movement of resistance and flight, by way of the Underground Railroad, that became widespread.[2]

Unfortunately, the historical accounts do not mention Nat Turner's brother Henderson Turner, or Henderson's two sons. Nor do they tell how Will and Adam Turner came to be sold to a plantation owner who apparently moved them to Marion County. I was never able to find out for sure on whose plantation in the Reddick area they were slaves.

I do remember Uncle Adam talking about Captain Rou's farm. There was a Samuel F. Rou, captain of the Marion Dragoons during the Confederacy, who owned a cotton plantation south of Reddick, near Lowell, in the 1850s. I can only speculate that he may have been the "Ol' Master" that Uncle Adam mentioned in his stories. Uncle Adam told of his days spent in slavery, how he worked in the fields from sunup to sundown every day. He had a smile as he told of the songs the slaves sang, songs with messages that the overseers couldn't understand. They would sing, "It's going to rain," when someone was about to get caught. "Couldn't hear nobody pray" meant to go ahead, that everything was going all right. The field hands would continue to work and watch for the boss man, for he said if they were caught not working they would be whipped and given extra work. The song "I cried and I cried" told the workers that they were in trouble. Uncle Adam said that they were happy people because they believed that Nat Turner and other brave slaves were making a way for them to be free. The stories were always sad but very interesting to me. We were all proud to know that we came down that family line.

At the end of the Civil War, times were tough for both the plantation owners and their freed slaves. Farmers no longer had laborers, and the former slaves had no paying jobs. Because of this, many of the freedmen made agreements with their former masters to continue to work on the farms as sharecroppers. In return, some former slaves were also deeded small parcels of land of their own.³ This may be how the Turner brothers came to acquire farming land in Reddick. I don't know how much land they were given, but it was several acres, mostly covered with trees. The brothers divided the land, giving some to their children as they became grown and got married. That is why the families all lived so close to one another.

Uncle Adam lived until 1929. When he died he was about 100 years old.

I enjoyed Papa's stories too. He used to take my brother and me along when he went to peddle fresh vegetables up in Hawthorne, which was northeast of Reddick. Traveling was always slow along the unpaved and sometimes ungraded roads. Along the way, Papa would talk about the memories of his own childhood.

Papa was born in Reddick on July 12, 1888, in a little log cabin with two rooms. He told us the cabin had only one window, a door, and a mud chimney—that's all. His mother, Grandma Vinie, wasn't married at the time, but after he was born she married J. T. Thompson, who became his stepdad, although Papa took his last name. Later, Grandma Vinie had sixteen more children with J. T. Thompson.

Papa told us the story of his first school experience. "When I was six years old, my mother sent me to school one day in Lowell, Florida, about four miles from home. An old lady had a school at some other people's house, and I went there with Bob Calvin's children. That night the children kept me over there at the Calvin's house, without telling Mama. Mama came and got me the next morning. She didn't know where I was that night, and she didn't send me to school anymore 'til I was ten years old."

He described to us the great freeze of 1895. His family was

living in the groves and picking oranges. A few days after the freeze, the ground was covered with oranges that had dropped off the trees. That spring they had to cut the trees down, drag them off, and plant cotton in their place.

Papa didn't have anybody to play with except some white boys. Malcolm Williams, as well as Bob, Frank, and Harley Bishop, would come down to his house while he was supposed to be babysitting his younger brothers and sisters. He told us how he would take the baby and they would all go out with their dogs and hunt rabbits. One evening when they came, it was just about the time the watermelons were getting ripe. They went through a neighbor's watermelon patch and busted one or two nice juicy red ones. The next day, Papa put the babies to sleep and headed over to the watermelon patch. He had to go right by the neighbor's gate, between the watermelon patch and his house. He didn't see anybody or look for anybody, so he went on into the watermelon patch and picked up a watermelon. Suddenly a man's voice hollered, "What' you doin' in my watermelon patch?" Papa dropped the watermelon, but there was no way to go home except right by his accuser. The man grabbed Papa and said, "Don't ever bother anybody else's things 'less they tell you."

"No, sir," Papa said. So from that day on he didn't steal or bother anything that didn't belong to him. He taught us children those same values that he learned as a boy.

One of Papa's most interesting stories was about the day lightning struck his house. Papa was home with the babies; his mother had carried the older children with her to the potato barn so they could learn about potatoes. Rain came, and it started thundering and lightning. Papa took his baby sister on his hip, the way he always carried her, and got a string to tie the door, which was swung outside. By the time he caught hold of the door, lightning struck the chimney and the house lit up.

The man next door had been standing on his kitchen porch and saw a bolt of lightning strike Papa's house. He told them later he thought they must all be dead. Papa grabbed the three children and went up to the man's house across the cotton patch. They stayed there until his mama came home, then they all went back to see the house. The rocks from the chimney were all over the room, from the chimney to the door. Part of the chimney was burning slow, and the door Papa was trying to shut was still swinging. He was nine years old.

Papa said they never did build that chimney back, and late that fall they went to stay with his mama's cousin, Rachel Turner. They stayed there two or three months through the winter, and that winter they had snow. It was the first time Papa had seen snow. The house had cracks in it at the top of the roof where there were homemade shingles, and snow was on the floor where it came through the cracks above.

Papa liked to talk about another incident that occurred while he was babysitting. It was in the spring, and he had been using an old plow handle to scratch up the ground near some hills of watermelon he was growing. His mama and Cousin Lou told him to watch their babies while they went to work. His mama's baby, Ruth, had been born about the same time as Cousin Lou's baby. So Papa put the babies to sleep.

While they were sleeping, Papa started teasing the dog with a bone. Papa had been told not to play with the dog, to let him catch possums, and it had caught one or two. The dog was under the house, and through the cracks Papa started tickling it with that bone. He was scared, because the dog's eyes showed green through the cracks under the house. While Papa was teasing the dog, Jakie came in, and he had that old plow handle in his hand. (Jakie was Papa's stepfather, Jake Thompson.) He started to beat Papa with it, and it split off onto the floor. When the handle broke, he stopped.

Then Jakie went off and met Papa's mama and Lou on the road. He told his mama, "I had to beat that ol' boy. I told him not to play with that dog no more."

When his mama got home she said, "Jakie told you to stop playing with that dog. Said he had to beat you. When I change my clothes, I'm going to beat you again."

After she changed her clothes, she sat down on the floor and told Papa to comb her hair. Then she noticed the knots he had on his thighs, knees, and arms from Jakie beating him. As Papa had told us, "He didn't knock the blood out of me, just left all those knots on me."

His mama said, "What are all them knots on you? Lou, come here, quick. Look where Jakie beat him." After she felt him all over she said, "I'm gonna find him and cut his throat." She went out, and after a while she came back. Papa said he didn't hear "no more 'bout it after that."

Papa said he went to school again from 1900 to 1904. He recalled that it was in 1904 that he was converted and baptized, establishing a faith that he carried with him the rest of his life.

As soon as he was sixteen years old, Papa persuaded his mother to take him out of school and bring him down to Wildwood to work. They were paying a dollar a day then, and Papa made thirty-one dollars in thirty-one days. He never did finish school, and maybe he regretted it, for he always stressed to us that his children would be educated.

Papa married in 1911. As his family grew, he became more and more active in his church and in the community. He served for many, many years as superintendent of Mount Olive Baptist Church, and later the United Baptist Church. He attended all of the local and state conventions, and never missed attending the National Baptist Convention, either. That responsibility gave him the opportunity to travel to many states in the Union, including Oklahoma and California, two that I remember. He would

Papa served for many years as Sunday-school superintendent at Mount Olive Baptist and later at the United Missionary Baptist Church of Reddick, shown in this 1998 photo. Mount Olive and Mount Cello Baptist Churches united and built this new building in 1976.

plan his days off from work, five days in the summer, so that he could go. The church paid his expenses. He would always bring back a report, and in this way the church kept up with the Sunday schools and other programs.

Papa was a great soloist, and he was called upon to sing for many occasions. Preachers would have him sing before their sermon, especially Reverend O. Van Pinkston, who was the moderator of the Baptist Congress in the second Bethlehem Association. Each year the program would call for the moderator's address, and Reverend Pinkston would always have Papa to sing. My, my, did those sisters shout and cry, "Sing Albert, sing!" Oh, those were happy days.

Papa was a quiet, serious-minded man; he did not joke around. He gave advice to the younger ones in our community, and it seemed that white and black, young and old, respected him. They called him Mr. Albert, or Deacon Thompson. He became the unofficial historian for our community. When people were interested in something that happened in Marion County, they would come to him and have him update them on it and when it happened. His memory was good up until the day he died, on January 17, 1990 at the age of 101. When asked a question he would pause and say, "Now let me see . . ." He would wait a few seconds and then begin to answer the question.

For several years, Papa was president of Reddick's Parent/ Teacher Association. He worked tirelessly in that capacity to persuade the Marion County school board to build a new school for black children in Reddick. Reverend C. P. Brown went with Papa and some other concerned citizens into Ocala to plead with the superintendent of schools. He helped organize the parents to conduct fundraisers. The women sold pies, box lunches, and other things in order to get the share of the money the community had to have to buy the land needed for a new school. Twenty acres of land on Church Street were ultimately purchased from a Mrs. Lushington, and Collier Elementary School was built in

Papa worked tirelessly to persuade the Marion County school board to build this school for blacks in Reddick. Collier Elementary was completed in 1929.

1929. The school was named after Dr. Nathan W. Collier, president of Florida Normal College in St. Augustine, a college that graduated many of Marion County's blacks (including my sisters Hettie, Thelma, and Eliza, as mentioned earlier). My brother, E. M., also attended Florida Normal College.

Reddick's black children attended Collier Elementary until the school system was integrated in the 1960s. Then Collier became the campus for lower elementary grades, and upper elementary students attended the formerly all-white Reddick school. In 1989 all students began attending Reddick Elementary, and the Collier school was closed.[4] Of course, this was heartbreaking to Papa and all the others who were old enough to remember what a struggle it had been to get a big, well-equipped school for blacks in our part of town. The Collier school building still stands and is used for other purposes today.

Reddick Elementary School for white children as it appeared in 1924. The school was later expanded and finally integrated in the 1960s. Photo courtesy of Louise Devore.

Papa helped support Florida Normal College in St. Augustine, shown in this 1920s photo of students in front of Anderson Hall. Hettie, Thelma, Eliza, and E. M. all furthered their education there. Photo courtesy of the Florida State Archives.

Papa was a serious, honest, hardworking man. He was well respected in Reddick, and people often went to him for advice.

Papa was also very involved with providing local support for Florida Normal College. The school began in 1918 as the Florida Baptist Academy, founded at Bethel Baptist Church in Jacksonville (my sister Hettie's church). Later it was moved to Live Oak and then to St. Augustine, and the named was changed to Florida Normal College. It was the responsibility of Baptist congregations throughout the state to provide ways to support the college. I remember when Papa would load up his truck with boxes of canned and dry goods collected from Marion County churches and carry them over to the college in St. Augustine. The school has since moved again, this time to Miami, and is now known as Florida Memorial College. The Baptist congregations still support the school with monetary gifts. Each year a day is set aside for contributions to be collected. I am the chairperson for donation day in my congregation today.

Papa may not have had a college education, but he certainly saw to it that others were educated. He was a serious, honest, hardworking man. Many people say I have all of Papa's ways.

CHAPTER 4

Reddick

MY HOMETOWN of Reddick was a small, close-knit farming community when I was growing up. Although it would never be described as prosperous, people, both black and white, were self-reliant for the most part. Those were the days of segregation, the days of WHITES ONLY signs in many places, but it seemed not to trouble anyone or cause any unrest in Reddick. The words "segregation," "integration," and even "racism" were not known to us. We respected the WHITES ONLY sign, and the sign COLORED meant that those doors belonged to us. At the railroad depot in Reddick, there was a small room on one side for us, and a larger room on the other side for whites. The water fountain outside the depot on the green had the sign WHITES ONLY, so we dared not use it, for we knew there would be severe punishment if a black drank from one of these marked fountains. We had our own separate hand pump, marked COLORED.

Everyone understood his place, and we were happy. People worked hard to make a living for their families, and blacks and whites alike were generous, lending a helping hand to those in need. We respected each other and were treated with respect. Blacks were welcome in all the stores in Reddick; there were no separate entrances. There were only a few public places where the separation was really apparent, mainly the churches and the schools.

There was one interracial "marriage" that I know of during the time I was growing up. One of north Marion's richest white men, Will Hull, and Uncle Adam's daughter, Lue Turner, lived together in Orange Lake. She may have been a housekeeper or a cook for him when the relationship began. I don't know for sure if they were married, but she used his name, and they had several children together who also had his name. I remember seeing them ride together past our house going to or from Uncle Adam's. Will Hull had a fine horse and buggy, and they made quite a stir, she with her very dark skin and he just as white as she was black, riding together through town that way. Papa told me a story about overhearing a salesman in the store say to Mr. Hull, teasing him, "How're them babies now?"

Well, Mr. Hull just hollered out to Lue in the buggy, "Lula, bring the baby in here." Then he sat that pretty baby proudly up on the counter just as if he didn't realize or care that they were making fun of him. I guess he got away with it because he was rich.

Most of the black community lived on the east side of Reddick, while whites lived on the west side. The only exceptions were Papa Ephraim, who as I said bought and lived in the old Reddick house; Mr. William Cabbaris; and Matthew Hart, a black farmer who had a large house not far from Joe Fanelli's. They were the only blacks living in what was considered the white neighborhood at the time. The first house built by and for blacks in Reddick was Mr. Cabbaris's house. Mr. Cabbaris had a small farm and in later years he and his wife ran a one-room shop on Dixie High-

William Cabarris's house was the first house built by and for blacks in Reddick. It still stands in this dilapidated condition.

way. They sold candies and ice cream. Mr. and Mrs. Cabbaris raised two daughters who both finished school and became teachers. Their original house still stands, although in a dilapidated condition, on the road to Matthew Hart's house. Mr. Hart's two-story block house was built sometime after his children were grown and started teaching. Matthew Hart, Jr., went to school at Bethune-Cookman at the same time I did, but instead of coming home in the summer he stayed and worked for Mrs. Bethune as a handyman. He became a teacher and later the principal of Belleview-Santos Elementary School in south Marion County. Children were expected to help out the family, and I'm sure that's how the Harts were able to build such a large house.

Dixie Highway (also referred to as Gainesville Road, Old State Road 441 or County Road 25A) was constructed with local limestone in the late 1800s. It was the main road between Ocala and

Matthew Hart's two-story block house was one of the few houses built by blacks in what was considered the white neighborhood at the time.

Gainesville and other points north. Paved in the early 1920s, it became a major truck route for transporting vegetables and fruits to northern markets.

Joe Fanelli's vegetable shed was a packinghouse where farmers would bring their crops to be sold, graded, and trucked away. Located on the east side of Dixie Highway, it was a large open structure where big trucks would come to pick up truckloads of vegetables bought from local farmers. Then they would take them to market in Jacksonville and other cities. Diagonally across the street from the vegetable shed was Mr. Fanelli's rock house, one of the prettiest houses in Reddick, and the only one built of stone. Surrounding the house was a two-foot-high rock wall that was very attractive. The house still stands today and is still owned and lived in by members of the Fanelli family.

The Reddick Supermarket, today the only grocery store in Reddick, was built on the site of Mr. Fanelli's vegetable shed.

Surrounded by a two-foot-high rock wall, Joe Fanelli's house was one of the prettiest homes in Reddick and the only one built of stone. It is still owned and lived in by members of the Fanelli family.

On the north side of Mr. Fanelli's house was the Redding Motor Company. Redding Motor Company was the first Ford automobile dealership in Marion County. Redding's Garage also sold batteries and gasoline, and did automobile mechanics work as well. That business didn't last long, for people weren't buying cars, especially during the Depression. Papa bought his first car, a Model T Ford, in Palmetto in 1921, the year Dorothy was born. He didn't know how to drive, and had to get a man to drive us

The Reddick Supermarket, today the only grocery store in the town, was built on the site of Mr. Fanelli's vegetable shed.

home to Reddick in it. Everyone in town, it seemed, both whites and blacks, crowded around to see Papa's new car. He was one of the first blacks in Reddick to own a car. He used it to take people into Ocala to shop, and we no longer had to walk to church on Sundays. Later on, Papa traded the Model T and got a truck for the farm.

The main commercial district in Reddick was located a few blocks east of the highway in the area surrounding the railroad depot. The depot itself sat just south of the railroad crossing. It was a long, wide wooden building, built high above the ground, with many wooden steps leading up to the platform. There was a walkway around the front and east side of the office where passenger trains would pull up for boarding. The colored waiting room had two or three long wooden benches and an iron stove for winter heat. The room had two windows, one on the side and the other in the front, next to the door. What was inside the other

Located on Dixie Highway, Redding's Garage was the first Ford dealership in Marion County. Photo courtesy of Louise Devore.

The Reddick depot, with a view of the pump house and the main business district, about 1920. Photo courtesy of Louise Devore.

waiting room I am not able to say, for we were not allowed in that room. The depot also housed a telegraph office and, in the south end of the building, a packing shed. Papa made boxes there during the summers. Several men and women worked under his direction, and he would train them how to make boxes. Shortly after integration our depot was moved to McIntosh, a little north of the town on Route 441, where today it houses an antique store.

Before the Great Depression, better known to us as the "Hoover days," there were several thriving businesses in what we called uptown Reddick. John and Alice Dupree owned a large wood-framed two-story boarding house across the railroad track on the northeast side of the depot. There was also a small store in the front of the building, with a single gas pump outside. The store sold mostly women's hats and other sundries, as well as trinkets. This is where Mama shopped for our Christmas gifts the year I found out there was no Santa Claus. Many salesmen and other travelers stayed at the boarding house on their way through Red-

The south end of the Reddick depot housed the telegraph office and a packing shed. Photo courtesy of Louise Devore.

dick. Boarders slept in the upstairs rooms and were served meals in a large dining room downstairs in the back part of the house. Mrs. Maggie Lewis, a gentle, well-respected black lady, was the housekeeper and cook. Mrs. Maggie would get others to help out with the work in the summer when travelers were many.

One year, when I was thirteen years old, she asked Mama if I could come and help in the kitchen. I did, and my job was to help wash dishes every day, Monday through Friday. It was my first paying job, and I earned fifty cents a week. From Mrs. Maggie I learned a lot about kitchen work.

Southern Peanut Products Company was a peanut butter factory located near the depot. It had a sign on its barrel of roasted peanuts that read, "Keep your d— hands out!"

There were seven stores in a row on the main street west of the depot. On the north end of the street was the Devore and Yongue

Mercantile, built adjoining the owner's house. The store sold dry goods and general merchandise. The next store was a meat market owned by John General, a black man. John General was the father of Blanche General, who later became a prominent educator in Broward County. Adjacent to the meat market was Ed Rou's general store. Papa Ephraim's market was next. He sold fish and beef as well as ice cream. Mama helped out in the store making the ice cream. John General's and Papa Ephraim's meat markets were the only stores run by black men. They were only open one day a week, on Saturdays.

Walking south past Papa Ephraim's market, one came to the Smith and Fridy dry goods stores. These general stores were open every day and sold a variety of dry goods and other merchandise such as cloth, hats, stockings, shoes, soap, flour, and sugar. There would be sacks of Northern White beans and barrels of rice. I remember that soap was five cents a bar. Mama shopped mainly in Fridy's store, as I recall. Most, and likely all of the stores, extended credit to their customers.

John and Alice Dupree owned a large two-story boardinghouse (*background, left*) that can be seen beyond the northeast side of the depot in this 1961 photo. Idella had her first paying job in the kitchen there when she was thirteen years old, earning fifty cents a week. Photo courtesy of Louise Devore.

Children sitting on the bench outside the Devore/Yongue Mercantile about 1920. Each store had an awning on the front. Photo courtesy of Louise Devore.

Ed Rou's general store housed the post office for a short time in the early 1900s. On the left, the side of Papa Ephraim's meat market can be seen. Photo courtesy of Louise Devore.

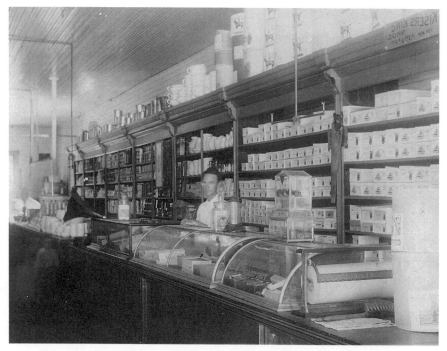

All of the general stores in Reddick had white owners. The stores were open every day and sold a variety of dry goods and other merchandise, such as cloth, hats, stockings, shoes, soap, flour, and sugar. Photo courtesy of Louise Devore.

There was a raised cement sidewalk that ran the length of the street in front of the row of stores. Each storefront had an awning or covered porch, with wooden benches in front of each store. We liked to sit on those benches and talk with friends while Mama shopped.

Oh, how we children loved to be sent into town for any sort of errand. It would give us a chance to visit with the friends we'd meet there. We could never stay long, though, for we had to get right back to Mama or Papa with whatever it was we were sent for. My cousin Lillie likes to tell the story of how Papa Ephraim would spit on the ground and tell her, "You'd better be back from the store before it [the spit] dries up."

In addition to the stores, Reddick also had a doctor's office and even a bank. The Reddick State Bank was a one-story red brick building that was built in 1923, a few years before the Depression. It was located on the main street north of the row of stores. Both whites and blacks did business there. The bank closed its doors in 1930 during the Depression and never reopened. Many people lost money, including Papa. The red brick building housed a branch of the Marion County Health Department until recently. It is now being renovated for some other use.

The combination doctor's office-and-drugstore was next to the bank on the corner, a small wood building. Dr. Wilson and later Dr. Gatrell served as physicians and druggists for the town. That building is still there, unoccupied at the moment. Around the corner from the doctor's office was a barbershop.

The first post office I remember was a wooden building next to Dupree's boarding house. It was replaced with a stone building that became known as the Little Rock Post Office. That building is still standing on the east side of the railroad right-of-way, across from where the depot once stood. In 1942 the post office moved

The Reddick State Bank, built in 1923, closed in 1930 during the Depression. The building later housed the post office, next a branch of the Marion County Health Department, and is now a sheriff's office substation. The building on the right was a combination doctor's office and drugstore.

Left: Currently a private residence, this building housed a barbershop when Idella was a child. It was located around the corner from the doctor's office, just off the main business district.

Center: The "Little Rock Post Office," built in 1914 next to Dupree's Boarding House, replaced an earlier wood post office building on the same site.
Bottom: The Reddick State Bank building housed the post office from 1942 until 1984.

to the former Reddick State Bank building, where it remained until a new post office building was constructed in 1984 on the east side of County Road 25A.

During the Great Depression, all of the businesses gradually closed down. Because many people were not able to get to Ocala to shop after the other stores closed, Mrs. Gutherie opened a little dry goods shop, which was our only store for a while. Mrs. Gutherie ran this shop, located next to her white two-story house on the east side of CR 25A. She also ran the only gas station, which had just one pump.

When the Voting Rights Act was passed in 1965, and we blacks were allowed to vote, it was in Mrs. Gutherie's store that we registered. I remember the day Papa said to me, "Come on. Let's go into Mrs. Gutherie's store and sign up to vote." This same place is where we went to cast our ballot on election day. Papa was our guide, telling the rest of the family that we were voting for such and such a one, and we would go in and mark an X by the name.

Built in the 1930s, Mrs. Gutherie's store on Highway 441 was the only store in Reddick after the others closed during the Depression. It was also the first polling place for blacks in Reddick. This photo was taken shortly before the building was torn down a few years ago.

Formerly a two-story building, Peter Brown's Hall was the only place blacks could go for entertainment when Idella was growing up. Because of its reputation of a rowdy "juke," Idella wasn't allowed to go there.

I didn't really know anything about who the politicians were, but Papa was very smart, and we children just voted the way he told us to. I don't know if there was anyone who influenced how he chose to vote.

About the only place in Reddick where blacks could go to dances, or to "have a good time," was a place called Peter Brown's Hall. Peter Brown had a large family of boys and the biggest farm owned by blacks in Reddick. He built the tall two-story building as a place for blacks to socialize. The dances were held upstairs, and food and most likely alcohol were sold downstairs. We called it the "Juke." It was located in a large field with a baseball diamond. Blacks would play baseball there on Saturdays. The Juke was only open on weekends.

Oh, how we children longed to go, if only once on the Fourth of July. We were never allowed to go there, of course, no, no, for Mama and Papa were very strict, and Peter Brown's Hall had a reputation of being a rowdy place. The so-called lower-class people went there. Someone was arrested at Peter Brown's Hall and put in jail just about every Saturday night, usually for fighting.

Reddick had a jail, a small wooden building with one cell. When blacks were arrested, that's where they went. We called it the "Calaboose." Whites were never put in the same jail cell with blacks; they must have been taken to Ocala when they were arrested. Court was held every Monday morning on Judge Cromartie's big front porch. In 1925, with Reddick's population of about 400, D. S. Cromartie was the mayor as well as the justice of the peace. He would decide if the accused had to pay a fine or spend another week in jail. The wooden jail was later replaced with a stone building across from the depot. That building is still there and is being used today as a private residence.

No, Peter Brown's Hall was off-limits for us, no matter how much we pleaded that all of our friends were going. When we

Now a private residence, this rock jail replaced an earlier wooden "calaboose" that often housed clientele from Peter Brown's Hall after a Saturday night brawl.

were teenagers, however, and thought we were grown, we did sometimes sneak there to watch a ball game. We never went inside the building and never went after dark, for we all had to be home before dark. I don't know if Mama ever found out that I went to the ball games, but if she did, she didn't whip me.

Various people through the years kept Peter Brown's Hall open after his death. Around 1960 the name was changed to Tim's Place; it was finally closed down for good sometime in the 1980s.

The only place our family went to socialize, besides school, was church. Church activities provided for a busy spiritual as well as social life for most of the citizens of Reddick, blacks and whites alike. There were two white churches in town, the Reddick Presbyterian Church and the Methodist church, both located on Colosseum Avenue, one block west of the business district. The blacks had four churches, Mount Cello Missionary Baptist Church on the west side of Dixie Highway, Mount Olive Baptist Church and a Methodist church, both on Church Street, and another Methodist church in East Reddick.

Mount Cello Missionary Baptist was the oldest black church in Reddick. Organized by a group of former slaves in the 1860s, the first meetings were held under a brush harbor in a place they called the "sink." In 1883, John M. Reddick deeded the land to the church for one dollar. In addition to being the meeting place, it became the site of Mount Cello Cemetery. The black community held services in a newly built log cabin and later a wooden building.[1] Eventually, a larger church building was constructed out on Dixie Highway, where it was located when I was a child. Grandma Vinie and all of her children except Papa were members there. We were members of the Mount Olive Baptist Church, located on a hill near the railroad on Church Street. Mount Olive was Papa Ephraim's church, and Papa went with him. Papa Jake, along with Mama's family, were members of the Methodist church on Church Street. The other Methodist church in East Reddick was pretty much made up of the members of one family who lived out there. I'm sure it began because it was too far for them to walk to one of the other churches. Mama started going to Mount Olive when she married Papa. Services were held on the first and third Sundays, with a circuit preacher from Inverness, Reverend Thompson, officiating. Reverend Rutledge held services at Mount Cello on the second and fourth Sundays. We attended there on those Sundays. All of the area congregations would join together for special events, such as fundraisers, Easter egg hunts, or parties. In 1976 the Mount Cello Missionary Baptist and Mount Olive Baptist congregations merged and built a new church building on the site of Mount Cello. The new church was named the United Missionary Baptist Church.

Idella looks down at her Mama's grave in Mount Cello Cemetery.

E. M. and Papa in front of Mount Olive Baptist Church, about 1943.

Before Papa got a horse and wagon, and later the car, we had to walk to church. We walked about two miles along the sandy, unpaved road from our house to the church. It took an hour.

Our family was very involved in the church and participated in all its activities. Papa was the head deacon and the Sunday school

Mount Zion United Methodist Church on Church Street, Mama's church before she married Papa, still stands today.

superintendent. The rest of the family sang in the choir, but I never could and still can't sing. Sunday school started at 10 A.M., followed by a long church service, which usually lasted until 2 P.M. Then from 4:30 to 5 P.M. there was a youth program, which we called BTU services. BTU stood for Baptist Training Union. The youth classes involved Bible study and memorizing verses. After that was night preaching, which lasted another hour. We stayed for it all. Going home, it was very dark walking. There were no streetlights, and we carried no lanterns. The only light to guide us was moonlight.

It bothered us that other children were allowed after morning church to go to the ice cream parlor across the street, while we had to stay with Mama and Papa at the church all day, between services eating the food we had carried in baskets from home. Mrs. Francis and her husband, Sam, started the ice cream parlor to provide a decent place for young people to gather. One could buy sandwiches, cold drinks, and ice cream there. When I was a teenager, Mama finally consented to let me go there between services. How I enjoyed meeting my friends, getting a cone, and talking outside. Later, after Mr. Sam's death, Mrs. Bell ran the shop so we could continue to have a place to go on Sunday afternoons. It was a treat we looked forward to after working all week and going to church every Sunday.

In 1951 a community center for blacks was completed on old Dixie Highway, north of town. Known as Club Charmant, it was built entirely with volunteer labor and donated supplies. Club Charmant was founded in 1946 by a group of young women who felt there was no type of social entertainment for young people to enjoy. Their husbands formed a separate club that met on the same day. They later combined the two groups into one. Thelma's husband, Alva, drew up the plans for the building. The men did all the work, while the wives brought dinner to the workers. As a nonprofit organization the club over the years has sponsored Boy Scouts and Girl Scouts, provided a lunch site for senior citizens, and provided a decent place for gatherings such as weddings, community socials, dances, and school activities. It is still in use today, celebrating its fifty-third anniversary in 1999. While the outside could use some sprucing up, the inside is lovely and well equipped.

Perhaps Club Charmant's most famous visitor was the actress Alfre Woodard, who played 'Geechee in the movie *Cross Creek*, which came out in 1983. She went with me to the club while she was "studying" for her part. The producers had called me from California and told me they were sending Miss Woodard ahead of the rest of the crew, and asked me if I would take her around. They wanted her to practice talking like me. When she arrived, she called me from the Howard Johnson's motel where she was staying. I picked her up there several times during the next week or so and drove her around in my car. I did most of the talking, as she was very quiet and didn't ask many questions. When the weekend came I thought about how our club was having its special anniversary program, and I asked her if she wanted to go. She agreed, and so I took her as my guest for the evening. Before we went she called to ask me how she should dress. I told her it was not fancy; it was in the country and dress was casual. So she wore a simple, long, cotton print dress, and I dressed simply too. I forgot that on our yearly anniversary night at the club, everyone dressed up.

The people at Club Charmant that night didn't really appreciate the importance of having Alfre Woodard as a guest. I guess in her plain clothes they all thought she was just another visitor. She wasn't well known yet; it was *Cross Creek* that really gave her career a boost. Only the youngest members knew about movie stars. One of them, Edna Simmons, struck up a conversation with her, and they seemed to hit it off well together. Edna invited her to her church, and after that Miss Woodard spent most of the rest

Built with volunteer labor and donated supplies in 1951, Club Charmant has provided a decent place for entertainment for almost fifty years. The black community center has sponsored many civic events, Boy and Girl Scouts meetings, clubs, dances, and other functions under the direction of its president, Philip Samuel. The actress Alfre Woodard visited here during the filming of the movie *Cross Creek*.

of her stay doing things with Edna. They became friends and continued to correspond for a while after the movie was finished. For my part, I was never offered and never received any compensation for the time I spent taking her around.

Though Reddick was mainly a farming town, there were other kinds of jobs that blacks could get. One such place was what was called the Lime Kettle. The Lime Kettle made cement blocks from lime that was mined in the area around Reddick. The Lime Kettle was located between East Reddick and Reddick proper. Wood was the fuel that kept the machines running. Some men worked cutting logs in the woods; others worked as truck drivers, taking the wood to the pit. There were four or five cottages, called quarters, for the workers and their families, as well as a commissary, where workers spent most of the money they earned on kerosene, beans, rice, or other necessities. They paid on credit, and ended up owing the store most of their salaries.

The old "Lime Kettle" provided jobs for many blacks in Reddick.

This 1913 photo of Florida Lime Company's plant in Zuber, a few miles south of Reddick, shows a similarity to the Reddick kiln when it was operational. Photo courtesy of the Florida State Archives.

This created a form of debt bondage that was common in other industries as well. The lime kiln operators would keep their workers in debt by overcharging them for provisions. Workers became entrapped in the system when they first came looking for work. Before they began work, they would often be offered credit at the commissary to cover their living expenses until payday came. Then their pay barely covered the debt, and they would have to be extended credit again. It wasn't much different from slavery, because workers could never break the cycle and get out of debt. Florida labor laws made it a crime for workers to leave the service of their employer if they had borrowed money or received goods with the promise to perform work for the company.[2]

Despite its drawbacks, working at the Lime Kettle did provide a continuous year-round job, not seasonal, like farming. Workers would say, when asked where they live, "I live to the Lime Kettle," a place where lime dust covered everything. My brother, E. M., worked there after school or on Saturdays, in the stockroom of the commissary.

Up until 1919 when the practice was outlawed, prisoners were used to provide local industries with cheap labor. The turpentine and lumber industries, railroads, and farms and mining industries all leased convict laborers during the years it was legal, from 1877 to 1919. This system made the debt-bondage cycle even worse, for when a worker tried to escape from an employer to whom he was indebted, he would be arrested and convicted of a crime. He would then become part of the prison work force, having to do the same work for no pay.[3] Fortunately, I was still very young when this practice ended, and I'm glad I have no memory of those cruel conditions.

Another place blacks could get work was at the "Side Camp." This was the place freight trains would stop on a sidetrack to be watered or serviced, and to let passenger trains go by on the main track. It was located two miles north of Reddick, near Millwood

This photo shows how men gathered "scrape," or pinesap, used in making turpentine. Photo courtesy of the Florida State Archives.

Blacks were often hired to do the grueling, hot, and dangerous work of distilling pine pitch to make turpentine and resin. This 1932 photo shows a Florida turpentine still, similar to the one that was located near the Side Camp in Reddick. Photo courtesy of the Florida State Archives.

Hettie, Mama, and Idella with Joyce Ann, the daughter E. M. never saw, standing in front of Mama and Papa's house. Idella was sitting on the unenclosed porch when Mrs. Rawlings drove up in the yard the first time.

Road. There were houses there for the workers too. Trains, once serviced at the Side Camp, continued on to Reddick, then past the section houses to Ocala. Along with the Side Camp there was a turpentine still, where pine pitch was distilled to make turpentine and resin. Pinesap would be brought from where it was collected in the surrounding pine forests. Pine trees were slashed in three or four V-shaped cuts on the trunk near the ground. Metal strips were hammered into the cuts to guide the sap as it ran. A pot placed under the V would collect the sap. At the turpentine still, workers fired and operated the machinery, then collected and stored the finished product. It was grueling, hot, and dangerous work.

On a big farm in East Reddick, about a quarter of a mile from Mama's house, Mr. Mayo owned and operated a grain silo and windmill, where men were hired to take care of the corn that was brought there to be ground. Mr. Mayo, a white man, raised fields of corn himself, but other farmers also took their corn to the silo to be ground and put into sacks. Papa always carried his corn to Fairfield, hauling it in our own wagon, pulled by our horse, George. He never took his corn to Mr. Mayo's silo, but he may have taken other farmers' corn there.

There were always jobs in the orange groves. Both blacks and whites were hired to do these jobs. Some men were truck drivers who picked up other workers and took them to the groves. Some worked at night to fire the groves in the winter; there was hoeing in the summer; and pickers were needed when the crop was ready. Other workers drove tractors with plows.

Mama and Papa's house as it looks today. It is the house where Marjorie Rawlings called for Idella in 1940, to hire her as a cook.

There was always something to do. Although salaries were low, jobs were available and black people worked.

In 1929 Papa built a house for our family. Papa Jake, Mama's father, gave us five acres of farmland, and Mr. Lewis, a carpenter friend of Papa's from Sparr, helped him build it. Completing it took a long time. When we first moved there, it was a long wooden house, one big open space with no divided rooms. It had a brick fireplace with a wide chimney in what eventually became the living room. There was a big porch, open and breezy. I remember the house was always cold, and we had to keep a fire going all the time. The driveway was on the left of the house. The yard had no grass and had to be raked constantly because of the leaves.

We lived that way, in one big room, for a year. Then, little by little, each year after he got his share of the crops, Papa would divide off another room. In all, when it was finished, there were eight rooms: kitchen, dining room, living room, and five bedrooms. Both Hettie and I were working by that time, and we helped Mama buy furniture for the house. Hettie bought a wicker couch for the living room, and I bought a dining-room set. Of course, we didn't have indoor plumbing; we had an outhouse. On the back porch, which was not screened, Papa divided off an area of privacy for the tin bathtub. We still used kerosene lamps for light, and added a portable kerosene heater made of tin. The house, which was eventually sold to friends from Fort Lauderdale, is still there. This is the house that Mrs. Marjorie Rawlings drove up to one day, calling for Idella Thompson. Little did I know how my life was about to change.

CHAPTER 5

Life with Marjorie
Kinnan Rawlings

T HE RECOLLECTIONS of my life with Marjorie Kinnan
Rawlings would take a long, long time to tell. Each time
I visit the Cross Creek house, I remember something else
that was said or done while I worked there. But never in my life
had I heard of Cross Creek until the day Mrs. Rawlings came to
my house in her beautiful cream-colored two-door Oldsmobile
with her big bird dog, Pat, sitting in the back seat.

I was twenty-six years old that October in 1940. Mama and all
of us children were sitting on the front porch. Rarely did a car of
any kind pass by our house, so we all took notice of this new-
looking car coming down the dirt road, never dreaming it would
turn into our driveway. The car came to a stop in the yard and,
windows down, the woman driving called out very clearly, "I'm
looking for Idella Thompson."

Mama and the other children stood there gazing, wondering
who it could be. I went down the porch steps and started toward
the car. I thought I knew who it was, for sometime that week I was

Mrs. Rawlings standing at the entrance to the grove at Cross Creek in 1939, shortly before Idella went to work for her. Photo courtesy of the Marjorie Kinnan Rawlings Collection, Department of Special Collections, George A. Smathers Libraries, University of Florida.

Idella, in West Palm Beach about 1939, shortly before going to work at Cross Creek.

expecting Mrs. Camp, a rich lady from Ocala, to come and talk to me about a cooking job I had inquired about.

I walked up to the driver's side window and said, "I'm Idella."

She asked, taking a cigarette out of her mouth, "Can you cook?"

Smiling, I said, "Yes ma'am, I am a good cook."

Without saying who she was, she got out her checkbook and began to write. With the cigarette back in her mouth, she passed me a check and began to talk very fast.

"Now Idella, I am going to be away in New York for about two weeks. Then I will come and pick you up. You see, I live in Cross Creek, about five miles from Island Grove."

The check, made out for two dollars, was now in my hand. I looked at it and saw the name "Rawlings," a name that meant nothing to me at the time. I said, "Oh, no, ma'am, I cannot work for you. I am going to work for Mrs. Camp in Ocala."

As the car began to move backwards, she said, "Oh, no. You don't want to work for that woman. She is too hard to get along with." With a wave, she and her dog were gone.

Mama immediately demanded, "What did that woman want?"

I was scared. Mama was the boss, and now her voice was very stern. I started to tell her what the woman had told me and about the check when she interrupted, "Let me see that check!"

I continued, saying, "She says she lives not too far from Island Grove."

While this was the first time I had heard of a place called Cross Creek, we had all long heard stories of Island Grove. I could visualize the old rugged wooden bridge just south of Island Grove and the curve in the road where the store and gas station were. We would pass by there when Papa took us to church conventions in Hawthorne, but we never stopped in Island Grove. Blacks never stopped there, for the story was that blacks were not welcome.

So Mama made the decision. "You are *not* going out there to work; those people will kill you. Give that check here." Mama took the check and where she put it, I don't know.

About a week later, I received in the mail another two-dollar check from Mrs. Rawlings. Mama took that one as well. She said, "When that lady comes I'll give them back to her."

I protested, "But Mama, she's already paid me for two weeks. I need to work for her at least that long."

Mama must have seen reason in that, because she said, "OK, get out your steamer trunk and put in a change of uniform. You can work your time out, but Sister, if they come after you out there, you get that trunk and you RUN!"

So I packed my oxford shoes, white socks, gray uniform with collar and cuffs, my cap and my apron: just enough for two weeks. I was ready to go when Mrs. Rawlings came for me.

It was a late afternoon, a few days later than she had said, that she arrived. We put my old steamer trunk into the trunk of her car. I opened the door and started to turn back the seat so I could climb in the back with her dog, Pat. She stopped me, saying, "Oh, no. Don't get back there; sit up here with me."

Well, don't you know I was scared! In those days blacks never rode up front with a white person; they always rode in the back. I didn't know what to think, but I did as she said. I stayed as close to the door as I could, with my hands in my lap the whole way to Cross Creek.

Though Reddick was in the country, the place we were going was even more so. The roads in the neighboring places, such as Orange Lake, Citra, and Island Grove, were mostly just one- or two-laned in the 1930s and 40s. Some were paved or graded, but many were unpaved. Traveling was slow no matter which route you took.

Mrs. Rawlings drove west on Church Street from our house to State Road 25A. From there she went north on 25A, a gravel road, to Orange Lake. She turned right on SR 318 and drove along a graded road to Citra. In Citra she turned left on US 301, a two-laned paved road, and drove north to Island Grove. She turned left at Island Grove on the narrow, deep sand road that would take us to Cross Creek.

Mrs. Rawlings didn't talk a lot during the trip. She would occasionally say things like, "Oh, isn't it a pretty day?" or "I'm glad you're going to work for me."

I talked even less, for I was scared, and I only answered, "Yes ma'am," and not much else.

After we turned onto the road to Cross Creek, I was overwhelmed with the beauty of the countryside. I saw only two houses just after the turn from Island Grove, then nothing but trees and bushes all the way to Cross Creek. I remember that the great magnolia trees were in full bloom. There were graceful palm trees, and many other flowering trees and bushes. Sometimes I exclaimed, "Oh, looka there," at a pretty sight, and Mrs. Rawlings would identify the tree or flower. She knew the names of all the plants.

The sun was setting when we arrived at the Cross Creek house, and the image was gorgeous. As the car bumped across the wooden cattle guard at the entrance of her driveway, Mrs. Rawlings said, "Well, Idella, here we are."

There were rows of blooming spider lilies on each side of the driveway, as high as the door handles of her car. On the right was the prettiest green lawn, planted in what must have been soft, winter rye grass. There were about four orange trees in this part of the yard, which Mrs. Rawlings called her young grove. There were low blooming petunias around the house and red and white flowers all along the fence line in front of the house. The front, with its bright green grass, reminded me of a well-kept golf course.

Oh, to me this was the loveliest country home I had ever seen.

Mrs. Rawlings' house at Cross Creek. Photo by Florida News Bureau, Department of Commerce, courtesy of the Marjorie Kinnan Rawlings Collection, Department of Special Collections, George A. Smathers Libraries, University of Florida.

The house appeared to have been freshly painted white, with dark green trim. "My, how pretty!" I exclaimed when I got out of the car. I must have had a big grin on my face.

Mrs. Rawlings said, "Idella, do you like it?"

"Lord, yes," I said.

A large tangerine tree stood just southwest of the carport, along with a palm tree. It was a wondrous sight—the big red sun sinking between the palm trees, surrounded by blue clouds. We just stood there gazing for a while.

Presently Mrs. Rawlings hollered out, "Yoo-hoo!" Several people came running from the back of the property. They turned out to be Miss Martha Mickins and her husband, Will, their son, called Little Will, and Little Will's girlfriend, Alberta. They called the younger Will "Little Will," but he was at least thirty years old when I first knew him. The group had come up from Miss Martha's house, where they all lived, and where I later learned I would be staying too. While they called it Miss Martha's house, it was really a tenant house that Mrs. Rawlings had on her property for her workers to live in.

Mrs. Rawlings introduced me this way: "Martha, this is Idella. She's going to be with us awhile. She'll stay in your house in that front room." She didn't tell Miss Martha that I would be taking her daughter Adrenna's place as cook. I later learned that Adrenna had left because she was going to have a baby, and Miss Martha had been helping in the kitchen.

Miss Martha just said, "Yes'm."

"Tomorrow morning you show her about the coffee," Mrs. Rawlings continued. To me she said, "Idella, Martha will show you about fixing the coffee."

"You know breakfast is at seven o'clock," Mrs. Rawlings added, addressing Martha again.

"Yes'm," replied Miss Martha.

Mrs. Rawlings told Little Will to get my trunk and Miss Martha to take me to my room. I couldn't see the tenant house from there, so I was shocked and disappointed when I was shown the old, unpainted wooden frame house that we, the workers, had to live in. A tin stovepipe came out of the north side of the house. An unscreened porch extended across the front of the house, with three steps leading up to it. The house was set on cement pillows, and the front of the building was much higher than the back. The front wall had a wooden door and a window. The door led to the front room, and behind it were two more rooms, a small kitchen, and a stoop on the back of the kitchen. On this stoop was a tin bucket, a dipper and a gourd, both used to dip water. There was a big round basin, used to wash face and hands. Long nails over the basin held the dipper and gourd. Not far from this bench were three large tin washtubs, which were used for the Mickenses' baths and for washing their clothes. My tub would be kept on the side of the front porch. There was a hand pump, which we all used to draw water. Under the side of the kitchen by Miss Martha's

LOW TO THE GROUND

There were three wooden Steps up to the porch.

Drawing of the TENANT HOUSE at
Cross Creek

Drawing of the tenant house at Cross Creek. Idella lived in this tiny house with the Mickenses. Her room was in the front, just off the porch.

room was a big water barrel. Water could be taken from this barrel for baths, and Miss Martha carried water from it to water her flowers. Water was also taken from the barrel when possible to boil clothes in the clothes pot.

Miss Martha showed me to my room, just off the front porch. It had just the one window, and was furnished with an army cot, a straight chair, and a small table with a lamp, wash basin and pitcher. There was a little wood-burning heater made of tin and a box for wood. The room had no ceiling, and you could see the tin top and rafters. The south wall had two or three long nails to hang my clothes on. There was neither a closet nor a dresser. A white sheet hanging in the doorway was all that separated my room from the Mickenses' room.

When I went to bed that night on that hard little cot, I had no dream of staying at Cross Creek beyond my two-week obligation. This was surely a big mistake, I thought, but it was only much later that I found out how it came about. I had recently returned to Reddick after working in West Palm Beach, and told some teacher friends that I believed I would stay home for a while. One of my friends, a teacher at the Collier School, told me his daddy worked as a chauffeur for a nice family in Ocala, the Camps, and that they were looking for a cook. So I went to the Camps' big house in Ocala, and went around to the back door and knocked. Someone yelled from the studio apartment over the carport, "Who is it? Come around here."

It turned out to be Bob Camp, Jr., and when I asked him if he was looking for a cook, he said, "Oh, no, that's my mommy. Mommy needs a cook. They're in North Carolina, but they'll be back in a week or two."

I gave him my name and credentials, as well as directions to my family's house in Reddick. He promised that his mother would come out to talk to me when they got back.

Well, it seems that Bob Camp's friend, Cecil Clark, had been in the room and had overheard. Cecil Clark, it turned out, was also a friend of Marjorie Rawlings, as were the Camps. Apparently, without telling Camp, Mr. Clark went right out to Cross Creek and told Mrs. Rawlings about me. That's how she happened to come looking for me that day. I heard later that when Mrs. Camp found out about it, she was plenty mad at Mrs. Rawlings and didn't speak to her for a long time. Then, after a while, Mrs. Camp, overdressed for the woods, came out to Cross Creek. She told Mrs. Rawlings, "I came out to see this 'Idella' you stole from me."

So that's how I happened to be where I was, looking up at the rafters of that old tenant house, never imagining I would stay with Mrs. Rawlings for ten years.

Before six the next morning, Miss Martha came in my room saying, "Baby, get up. It's time. Hurry up; she has to have her breakfast at seven o'clock."

I noticed a large banana plant next to the kitchen door as we went inside Mrs. Rawlings' house. Miss Martha started a fire in the stove and then took great pride in showing me how to fix the coffee. I thought to myself, Often as I've done it, I think I know how to make coffee.

She put clean, mashed-up eggshells in the bottom of the ceramic pot along with the ground coffee. The eggshells, she explained importantly, help to settle the coffee. As she worked, she explained how "Missy," as she called Mrs. Rawlings, liked her breakfast tray fixed.

When it was ready, we carried the tray to Mrs. Rawlings' room. The tray held Mrs. Rawlings' typical breakfast: a soft, three-minute boiled egg, buttered toast and jelly, coffee, and fresh-squeezed juice. Also on the tray were a vase with a fresh-cut flower and a plate of cat food for Mrs. Rawlings' Siamese kitten, Smokey.

Miss Martha set the tray on a chair while she put a backrest pillow behind Mrs. Rawlings. Then she put the tray in front of her. Smokey, the cat that had been curled up on the bed, ate off the same tray as Mrs. Rawlings did.

I noticed the room was quite cool. As Miss Martha started a fire in the fireplace, I said to myself, I'd have thought she'd have started the fire first.

Mrs. Rawlings said, "Martha, I'll take care of showing Idella around after lunch." And for about the first week, Mrs. Rawlings and I worked together on how to fix meals. I remember that first night for dinner we had lamb chops, baked potato, and salad. Mrs. Rawlings didn't do any writing the first week I was there. Miss Martha helped me with breakfast and lunch, and Mrs. Rawlings showed me about dinner. When she wasn't working with me,

Mrs. Rawlings would go out on the porch to read. She loved to read as much as she loved to write, and was always receiving a new book that I would find stuffed in the mailbox by the gate when I went out to get her mail.

One morning I was standing by her bookcase looking at her books. Mrs. Rawlings came in unexpectedly with a loud, "Good morning," and caught me with one of her books in my hand. I was scared, thinking she would fuss at me because I was touching her things instead of dusting. Instead, as I was replacing the book on the shelf, she asked, "Idella, can you read?"

I answered, "Yes, I can read."

"Do you like to read? Have you seen my books?"

"Your books?" I asked, surprised.

Mrs. Rawlings pulled two books off the shelves, *The Yearling* and *South Moon Under*. "Didn't you know I'm a writer?"

"Oh," I replied. Now I knew she wasn't mad at me.

"You can take a book home with you at night to read if you want to," she told me. "Would you like that?"

So from then on I borrowed Mrs. Rawlings' books to read. I always let her know which one I had.

From my first day at Cross Creek, Mrs. Rawlings had carefully instructed me not to bother her table and not to empty the wastebasket by it. There were always wads of paper on and around the table, on the floor or in that wastebasket. Learning that she was a writer finally made it clear to me why she didn't want me to clean up that mess.

I took it upon myself to protect Mrs. Rawlings from being interrupted while she was working. She had begun work on the book *Cross Creek*. I wouldn't let any of the other help bother her, and I would stop curious visitors before they could get to the house. Tourists would come to Cross Creek hoping to get a glimpse of the famous writer. Some were so bold as to walk right in the yard and peer through the screens. If they got to Mrs.

Rawlings, she would feel obligated to greet them and sign auto-graphs, so I did my best to keep them away. Mrs. Rawlings told me how much she appreciated it, and she always let me know if she was expecting someone and that it was okay to let him or her in.

It wasn't long before I discovered that I enjoyed this job, and I was fascinated with Mrs. Rawlings the writer. I was interested in the things she talked about, her knowledge, and the people she knew. But what really clinched it for me, I think, was when Satur-day came and she told Little Will, Alberta, and me to take her truck and go have a good time. When I found out from Will that she allowed this every Saturday, the idea of that kind of freedom made me want to keep this job. So I had Little Will take me home to Reddick so I could get some more clothes, for I still only had one change of uniform with me.

Mama didn't comment when I told her I was staying on with Mrs. Rawlings. I think she was relieved to know that I could come home on the weekends and that I wasn't stuck at Cross Creek without any way out. Of course, I didn't tell her that we were all going out somewhere for a "good time." I soon found out that when it comes to having a good time, Little Will and Alberta didn't speak the same English I did. We went to Boardman, the black community just north of McIntosh, and went jukin'. "Jukin'" was what mostly lower-class blacks did for entertainment at the end of a long workweek. Each Saturday the "jukes" were filled with men and women who were going out for a night on the town, and believe me, they would make it a night. Under-age children would try to get in and often did, because they didn't really check for I.D.s in those days. There were juke joints all over, on Broadway in Ocala, one in Citra, and of course, Peter Brown's Hall in Reddick. Some, like Dr. Lamb's place in west Ocala, were for the "higher ups." One man jokingly said this was where the "big dogs" go, meaning the higher class of blacks. Peter

Brown's, the Boardman Juke, Citra and others were for the "little dogs." At a juke joint you would hear the most unbecoming language and loud cussing, and there would almost always be fights breaking out, some of them ending in murder. Beer and hard liquor were sold and consumed, and there would be dancing all night long. No sir, "jukin'" with the drinking, cussing and fighting associated with it was just not my type of entertainment. So from then on, I would have Little Will drop me off at Mama's on Saturday and come back for me on his way back to Cross Creek.

One day awhile later, Mrs. Rawlings told me that her best friend, Julia Scribner, was coming for a visit, and she had me clean the guest room up for her. Miss Julia was the daughter of Charles Scribner, Mrs. Rawlings' publisher. On the morning Miss Julia was to arrive, I carried Mrs. Rawlings' breakfast tray into her bedroom as usual. Mrs. Rawlings was sitting up in bed, but her face was so bright red that I was alarmed. I set the breakfast tray on the floor and exclaimed, "Mrs. Rawlings, what's the matter?" Mrs. Rawlings was nearly in tears.

"Oh, Idella, I was sick all night." I soon learned that Mrs. Rawlings had these spells quite often, and have since found out that they were severe attacks of diverticulitis. Diverticula are small tubular sacs that develop along the wall of the intestine, especially the colon. This condition is known as diverticulosis and causes no problem until the sacs become inflamed or infected, causing symptoms that can include severe pain, nausea, vomiting, or diarrhea.[1] Mrs. Rawlings wrote this to Max Perkins, her editor, about her condition in 1938: "After a series of X-rays, I have finally run down the source of a condition that has kept me half-sick all my life. . . . There is a mass of twenty-five or thirty diverticulae."[2] She was concerned at that time that she was going to have to have part of her intestines removed, but doctors later decided to treat the condition with diet and medication.

This time she was in obvious pain, but she was most concerned about Miss Julia's arrival.

"Julia's coming on the train this morning. I was supposed to meet her at 9:30. I can't go get her like this," she cried. "It won't do to have Will pick her up in that truck, and I'm damn sure not going to let him drive my car."

"I'll go get her," I offered.

"You know how to drive?" she asked.

"Yes ma'am, I can drive," I said.

"You can drive? You've got a license? Go get it!"

I knew how to drive, for Papa had taught me, but I also had a license by that time. Once when visiting family friends in West Palm Beach, a friend was going to get his license and suggested I come get one too. In those days, all you had to do was fill out a form to get a driver's license. There wasn't any written test or driving test, not even a vision test. So that's how I happened to have a driver's license, a little green paper with my name but no picture on it.

When Mrs. Rawlings told me to get it, I went flying down to the tenant house as fast as I could and brought back my driver's license to show her. When she saw it she said, "All right. Thank God. Go and get Julia."

"But I don't know Miss Julia," I told her.

"That's all right," she said. "Just stand there and holler her name at the train."

So I struck out for Gainesville in Mrs. Rawlings' Oldsmobile. In those days there were separate coaches for whites and blacks, so I stood by the white coach and said, "Miss Julia," loudly, every time a lady got off the train. I got a lot of funny looks before a nice-looking young woman wearing a pantsuit answered me, saying, "Hi, I'm Julia. Are you Idella? Where's Marge?" I told her that Mrs. Rawlings was sick, and we loaded up her luggage and I headed back to Cross Creek. When we arrived, Miss Julia ran straight to Mrs. Rawlings's room and asked, "What's the matter?" Mrs. Rawlings made light of her illness, saying it was just a virus, "I'll be all right soon."

From then on, I was driving, and Mrs. Rawlings let me take her car on Saturdays when I went to visit my family in Reddick. I could keep the car all weekend and only had to be back in time for breakfast on Monday morning. In fact, I could use her car any time she did not need it. Often I was called upon to run errands that required me to take Mrs. Rawlings' car into Ocala or Gainesville. It was a great feeling for me, driving that new-looking, cream-colored Oldsmobile.

After about the first two weeks at Cross Creek, I told Mrs. Rawlings, "I don't need Miss Martha now." So Miss Martha was excused from the kitchen, and I did the cooking from then on. Mrs. Rawlings would tell me to make a menu, so I would suggest we have such and such this day, and I enjoyed that. She might say, "All right, that sounds good, make it." Or, if she had something else in mind, she'd say, "Why don't we have this or that?" I baked bread at least twice a week and rolls if company was coming. We hardly ever bought bread.

When I wasn't cooking I was cleaning. The cleaning had really been neglected while Miss Martha was in charge, and the house needed a thorough going-over when I arrived. I brushed down cobwebs, and dusted and polished everything. The bare, unpainted wood floors had to be scrubbed daily, especially those in the kitchen and bathrooms. This was done on my hands and knees with a bucket of water with lye soap and a scrub brush. They didn't use mops in those days. I wore my uniforms all the time, usually changing in the afternoon before serving the evening meal. In a letter Mrs. Rawlings wrote to a friend in June of 1941, she described me this way: "She [Idella] is the answer to a prayer. Not only a marvelous cook, but doesn't drink, isn't interested in men, borrows my books, likes the same movies I do, and adores having company and protests when I pay her extra after a heavy week. Her cheerfulness and efficiency are balm after the wounds Martha and Adrenna inflicted on me."[3]

Of course, I didn't read that until sometime after her death, and when I did my friends and I had quite a laugh. My friends told me, "She's sure got the wrong Idella. I can tell she didn't know you." It was true; the only reason she got me was because I was running away from a man at the time.

While I was working for the Bowens in West Palm Beach, I had gotten involved with a boyfriend. He was a nice-looking man from Nassau, the Bahamas, always neatly dressed in expensive clothes and shined shoes. Well, I found out that what was apparently customary between couples in Nassau was not the same custom in Reddick. I'm telling you I got scared of that man, 'cause I knew I wasn't doing right. We had a big misunderstanding, and I had to get away. I was afraid of him—that he would get a hold of me—so the very next day I packed my things and got a friend to drive me home to Reddick, where I was sure he wouldn't follow me. I sent a letter to the Bowens explaining only that I had to return to my family, without telling them the real reason. The Bowens weren't mad, and they kept in touch for several years. Mrs. Bowen sent me a Bible for Christmas in 1942. That was the last gift I received from her, but they visited me in Reddick once many years later, after I had left Mrs. Rawlings.

Mrs. Rawlings never knew it, but after I'd been there awhile I invited guests, both men and women, to visit me at Cross Creek in the evening after work. They'd come over the cattle guard and follow the road around back to the tenant house. Sometimes we'd go out and return late.

What Mrs. Rawlings said about the drinking was true; I did not drink. I was teased about it at Cross Creek. When Mrs. Rawlings was entertaining guests, she would often have Miss Martha and the others entertain them with music. Miss Martha had a lovely

The staff entertains guests at Cross Creek at a party in 1940. *Standing, left to right:* Sissie Fountain, Alberta, Henry Fountain, Martha Mickens, and Little Will Mickens. *Seated, left to right:* Cecil Clark, Norton Baskin, Marjorie Kinnan Rawlings, and state senator Verle Pope. Photo courtesy of the Marjorie Kinnan Rawlings Collection, Department of Special Collections, George A. Smathers Libraries, University of Florida.

Martha and Will Mickens, standing in the yard at Cross Creek. Photo courtesy of the Marjorie Kinnan Rawlings Collection, Department of Special Collections, George A. Smathers Libraries, University of Florida.

voice and liked to sing rousing old spirituals. The liquor would flow freely to all during these times. I would be sitting out on the porch while they sang and had fun. I would hear Mrs. Rawlings holler, "Get Idella some water. She doesn't drink," and everyone would laugh. I would be mad, because I had to wait until the drinking and singing was over before I could serve dinner.

Miss Martha—when I got to know her—was a lovely woman. It was obvious that she loved, cared for, and would do anything for, Mrs. Rawlings. She once said to me, "Baby, you don't know. Me and her have been through many things." She was referring, I'm sure, to the difficult times Mrs. Rawlings had had as she struggled to make a living before she sold her first book. By the time I arrived, Mrs. Rawlings had some money, for she had just sold the movie rights to her book *The Yearling*.

Miss Martha was considered a jack-of-all-trades, but her main responsibility was to do Mrs. Rawlings' laundry every Monday. She also kept an eye on the house and helped out with other chores when needed. She had helped Mrs. Rawlings when she

Outside the back porch at Cross Creek in 1941. *Left to right:* Martha Mickens, Alberta, Idella, and Little Will. Photo courtesy of the Marjorie Kinnan Rawlings Collection, Department of Special Collections, George A. Smathers Libraries, University of Florida.

was struggling, and her place was secure at Cross Creek. When Mrs. Rawlings told Martha that God had sent her a perfect maid—meaning me—Martha snorted, "Well sugar, God sets high but sure look low."

Miss Martha's husband, Will Mickens, was another matter. He was a man who I never saw do any type of work. Mrs. Rawlings said she would have gotten Will out of that place, but she knew Miss Martha would follow him. So he remained, and to me, he was the meddler of the place. He would sit on the porch and watch the cars, taking note of who came or went from Cross Creek. If he saw a lot of people at the house, he would ask me, "Cook, what's Old Miss doing up there?"

Little Will's duties included keeping the woodbin full, and keeping a supply of newspaper used to start the kindling. He also milked Mrs. Rawlings' cow, Dora, and fed her and the bull, Ferdinand. In addition, he tended the yard. When young Will was gone on a drinking binge for a few days, Miss Martha took over his chores. Mrs. Rawlings knew Little Will went on these drunks, but she didn't mind as long as the work was done. Little Will's girlfriend, Alberta, tended the flower gardens.

Miss Martha had another daughter, Sissie, who lived at Cross Creek with her husband, Henry Fountain, and their five children. They lived around the bend, not far from the bridge, in a run-down house. I never went there, but I was told it was near the Basses' house. The Basses were a poor white family who lived at the Creek. Henry Fountain was slightly disabled and was not able to work. The family was very poor, and Martha must have helped them get by.

One summer some time later, Mrs. Rawlings took a liking to one of Sissie's little girls, named Martha after her grandmother. Little Martha was a cute, soft-haired girl with a sheepish smile. Mrs. Rawlings asked Sissie to let Little Martha, who was about three or four years old at the time, live with her at Crescent

Beach. Well, she took Little Martha to Crescent Beach, but not to stay with her, for these were still the 1940s. Oh, sure, the cute little black girl, who Mrs. Rawlings asked to live with her, was given over to live with Idella. I didn't mind too much, for she was company for me.

Everywhere I went with Mrs. Rawlings, I was isolated. Mrs. Rawlings' cottage at Crescent Beach was much smaller than the house at Cross Creek. Consequently Mrs. Rawlings had fewer guests there. When we went to the beach it was almost like a vacation for me. The floors were painted and much easier to keep clean. Since my responsibilities were fewer, I had almost every afternoon off. That summer I spent the time teaching Little Martha and sewing little dresses for her. Mrs. Rawlings gave me money to buy the cloth. When we got home to Cross Creek at the end of the summer, all the other children circled around Little Martha with her pretty dresses and her hair all done up. But Little Martha had been homesick the whole summer, repeatedly asking me when we were going back to Cross Creek. She had no other children to play with all summer at Crescent Beach, having no company except Mrs. Rawlings and me. She missed her brothers and sisters, so when she got home, she was determined to stay home. She refused to go back to Mrs. Rawlings, and so that was the end of that.

It wasn't until after Mrs. Rawlings' death, when her letters were released, that I read what she wrote about me that summer. Apparently I had misspelled a word on the grocery list I had given her when she was going to town. She wrote something to the effect that there I was trying to teach Little Martha correct English and I couldn't even spell the word *lemon*, or whatever the misspelled word was. She also made a comment about the inadequacies of education for blacks.[4] I learned a lot more about who Mrs. Rawlings was after I read her letters.

Miss Martha's family and I were the only blacks living in Cross

Creek that I know of. If any of Mrs. Rawlings' four neighbors had black help, I never knew it. There was never time to go visiting, even if there had been people to visit.

Mrs. Rawlings also had some white workers helping her at Cross Creek. Mr. Chet Crosby, or Mr. Chet, as we were told to call him, was the grove manager. He was the boss of the grove workers. There was Snow Slater, who we just called Snow. He was the fellow who drove the tractor and kept the groves plowed. He also helped with the firing of the grove heaters and bedded the trees in the winter when there was a freeze. Trees were bedded by piling dirt up around the base of the tree above the graft. That way, if the tree froze, it would grow back from the graft and not from the sour orange roots.

Mr. Fiddia (pronounced Fiddy) lived in the scrubs, I think, out where the story *The Yearling* took place, near Salt Springs. He was what Mrs. Rawlings called her "all-'round man." He would come all the way from Salt Springs and do some of everything, including fix things around the place that were broken.

I don't know much about Mrs. Rawlings' four neighbors, besides their names. They were the Williamses, the Bass family, Jake Glisson, and Mr. Brice. Mrs. Rawlings didn't spend any time visiting her neighbors, unless there was a death in the family or some sickness, but sometimes they would come to her.

Her closest neighbor, Mr. Brice, was the one she talked with more often than with any of the others. I would see her talking to him over the fence from time to time. Mr. Brice was called the "boss" of Cross Creek. Will Mickens, who as I said before was a meddler, said to me once, "Well, before Old Miss came to Cross Creek, old man Brice was the boss, but now Old Miss is the boss. I believe that is what all the confusion is about."

I asked, "What confusion?"

"Oh, Cook, don't you know whenever they have something to settle, all of them go down to the creek and have their meeting?"

"No, Mr. Will," I replied. "I did not know that."

In truth, I did know that they went to the bridge sometimes to talk and settle disputes, as was the custom for feuding neighbors to do in Cross Creek,[5] but I can't say any more than that from first-hand knowledge, for I certainly was never with them. However, Mrs. Rawlings did describe in one of her letters a conflict that was settled that way. The dispute was apparently between the Brices and the Glissons over who should pay for two cattle gaps on right-of-way land the Glissons had leased to the Brices. A cattle gap is a sort of wooden bridge built at an opening in a fence to prevent hoofed animals from crossing. The boards are widely spaced, so that a cow would be afraid to step there because its hooves would fall between the boards. To settle the controversy, Mrs. Rawlings offered to pay for one of the cattle gaps herself, and Tom Glisson would pay for the other.[6] I can imagine that she was the peacemaker in many such disputes.

Mrs. Rawlings always helped out the poor families at the Creek, especially at Christmas. She bought clothes for Sissie's children and for the Bass children, and Buddy (Ernest) Bass especially remembers her bringing bags of candy, even expensive chocolates from New York, at Christmastime. For the grown-ups she bought bottles of Seagram's 7 whiskey. Mrs. Rawlings helped out the Bass family significantly by helping to finance a little restaurant in their home. At a recent Rawlings Society conference, Buddy Bass told the story of the time Mrs. Rawlings came and ate catfish at their restaurant, and then asked his parents if she could take eleven-year-old Buddy home with her. Buddy visited for ten days and has fond memories of Mrs. Rawlings reading to him and taking him to Belks in Ocala to buy new clothes.

It's strange to me how in those early days at Cross Creek we knew it wasn't slavery; but our life there must have been similar to plantation life. We lived crowded in the small, unpainted, tin-top tenant house, with little comforts. We had to do what we were told, and we were isolated from other people. We couldn't leave the place unless Mrs. Rawlings let us use her car or truck, and we were always told what time to be back. The only difference between that and slavery, I think, was that the slaves were not paid like we were.

There's no single reason I decided to stay with Mrs. Rawlings. It was a good job for the times, when jobs were hard to find, and two dollars a week was top wages for blacks. It may have been because I was allowed to drive Mrs. Rawlings' new car as if it were mine, or because I got to travel to places I never would have otherwise visited.

Mrs. Rawlings, I came to find, was not one to stay in one place for very long. She got restless and at a moment's notice would announce she was going somewhere. I would have to pack our things in a hurry and be ready to go.

I remember the time she went to Blowing Rock, North Carolina, to visit friends and do some writing. It was to be my first time ever seeing mountains, and I was excited and looking forward to it. She and I took turns driving, and when we got there Mrs. Rawlings had to find a place for me to stay. She drove into the black part of town and left me at a rooming house while she went on to stay with her friends, the Lyonses from the University of Florida, who had a home there. My room was very untidy, and I'd never seen so many bugs in one place in my life as I saw that night. I was very glad to see Mrs. Rawlings when she picked me up the next morning. She had rented a cottage up on top of the mountain, where she planned to spend some time writing. I drove with a lot of trepidation up that steep and curvy road as it wound up the side of the mountain. Once at the top, I remember I couldn't sleep that first night, wondering how in the world I would get back down that crooked road. When the time came to descend, I discovered my fears were unfounded; it was not so bad going down after all.

Idella (*right*) and Martha Mickens preparing for a dinner party in the kitchen at Cross Creek about 1940. Photo courtesy of the Marjorie Kinnan Rawlings Collection, Department of Special Collections, George A. Smathers Libraries, University of Florida.

All that traveling was new and exciting to me, and it was a plea-sure to be able to serve the famous or important people who came to Cross Creek to visit. I do think that if it had not been for those things, I would not have stayed as long as I did.

But stay I did, against Mama's wishes, and as time went by, I began to love Cross Creek and the other places we lived during the year.

Today, I can say that working at Cross Creek didn't seem hard. I enjoyed cooking, and I was given the freedom to experiment with ingredients, without fear of wasting anything. If something didn't come out just right, Mrs. Rawlings would go to the store for more supplies until we got it right. At home in Reddick, I would have had to be careful, because we did not have the money to go to the store whenever we ran out of things. So it was luxury to be in that kitchen and cook. A lot of my cooking was done with a pinch of this or a dash of that, while in the kitchen as we were working on recipes for her book *Cross Creek Cookery*, she would often say, "Now Idella, it must come out right. Let's start the measurements all over again." We did this many times until each recipe was correct.

It was a joy serving her guests and hearing them exclaim over the different dishes, asking, "Marge, how did you fix this?" Some-times she would call me and ask, or other times Mrs. Rawlings would say that she had put this or that in it. It didn't matter too much to me that I didn't get the credit. Both Mrs. Rawlings and I were good cooks, and we enjoyed and often worked together on planning and cooking the meals.

What delight I would have when Mrs. Rawlings would say that Mrs. Margaret Mitchell, or some other famous person, was com-ing for dinner. She might say, "My publisher's daughter will be here." At first the names meant nothing to me, for in my limited experience I had never heard of them and didn't know they were famous. It never occurred to me to ask for their autographs when

Margaret Mitchell (*left*) and Marjorie Kinnan Rawlings. Photo courtesy of the Marjorie Kinnan Rawlings Collection, Department of Special Collections, George A. Smathers Libraries, University of Florida.

they were there. During my first year at Cross Creek they were filming the movie *The Yearling*. Mrs. Rawlings would invite the cast and crew to the house for dinner. I served people such as Spencer Tracy, who was first chosen to play the lead, and Gregory Peck, who was ultimately given the part. Mrs. Rawlings would have to tell me who they were and why they were significant. Just to be able to serve people I had heard about, or those mentioned as doing this or that, was a pleasure. Those were happy days for me.

Even when Mrs. Rawlings wasn't having guests, I would still have to prepare a complete dinner for her. It seemed a waste to cook a whole roast beef for just the two of us, but we did it. She usually took her dinner in the dining room, and I would serve her each course just as I did when guests were there. Then I would go in the kitchen to eat my dinner. Even though it was only the two of us, I still had my place as servant; she never once invited me to sit at the table with her to eat. She was more relaxed with me when we were alone, however. It was different when company was there. That's when I was really treated as a servant. Mrs. Rawlings wanted everything to be just right and would some-times bark orders at me throughout such a visit. I remember once I was slow (so she thought) bringing in the hot biscuits to the table. Mrs. Rawlings yelled for me in front of the guests. Then, as I was coming through the swinging door, she jumped up from her seat and snatched the biscuits out of my hands. "Why the hell didn't you hurry up with the food?" she hollered. She wouldn't have done that if she hadn't had company, I believe.

I know people would love for me to tell about the visits of fa-mous writers and other dignitaries to Cross Creek and the Cres-cent Beach house. I wish I knew then what I know now about them, for I sure would have paid better attention. But one has to remember that in those days I was a servant. Most of the time Mrs. Rawlings didn't take the time to even introduce me to her guests, and when she did, they were just names. I recall the names, but I think Ernest Hemingway was the only name I recognized at the time. I did take a little scrap of paper and ask him to put his name on it. I don't know where in the world I put that autograph, for I don't have it today.

I'll never forget the time Mrs. Rawlings loaned the Cross Creek house for a week to Mrs. Marcia Davenport, her writer friend from New York. Mrs. Rawlings was not there, but I was "loaned" also as cook and housekeeper for Mrs. Davenport and her friend while they were on vacation. Mrs. Rawlings instructed me to call the man Mr. John. I, in turn, had Miss Martha and the other workers call him Mr. John, for that's what I thought his name was. Mrs. Davenport and Mr. John seemed to enjoy the stillness out at

Marcia Davenport, 1944. A pretty lady with a charming voice, Mrs. Davenport was one of the loveliest people Idella met during her years with Mrs. Rawlings. Photo by Halsman Photographers, used at the Marjorie Kinnan Rawlings Collection, Department of Special Collections, George A. Smathers Libraries, University of Florida.

the Creek. I could not half-understand Mr. John's speech, for he had a thick accent. He loved to watch the Mallard ducks from the back porch, and I remember he would remark how pretty the "dooks" were. I really enjoyed their company that week.

Then, one awful morning a short time after their visit, I went out to the paper box at the end of the driveway and got the morning newspaper, the *Gainesville Sun*. I couldn't believe it—there on the front page was a picture of "Mr. John," along with the news that he had been killed in a fall from a hotel window! I started running and crying, calling Mrs. Rawlings. She came swiftly to the front door, saying, "Idella, Idella, what's the matter?"

"Mrs. Rawlings," I cried, "Mr. John is dead!" "Mr. John," it turned out, was Jan Masaryk, the Czechoslovakian foreign minister. Mrs. Rawlings and I shared our sorrow together as she read the newspaper report.

About four years ago a lady came up to me at a Marjorie Kinnan

Rawlings Society meeting and told me she had visited Mrs. Davenport, who lived somewhere outside the country. She said they had talked about me, and Mrs. Davenport asked if I was still alive. Last year I was saddened to hear of her passing, for I thought she was one of the loveliest people I had ever met during my years with Mrs. Rawlings. I named my niece Marcia for her. I wanted always to remember this pretty lady with the charming voice.

One thing that seemed strange to me was that Mrs. Rawlings seemed to prefer the company of men to that of women. I prepared more breakfasts, dinners, and snacks for men visitors than for women. Once, on a few hours notice, I was told to get a complete dinner ready for ten men. No, no, not one woman. There wasn't ever a ladies' luncheon or a ladies' bridge party. These things seemed odd, but I never questioned them. Of course, some

Idella and Miss Dessie, taken in April 1998 at the MKR Society Convention in St. Augustine.

of Mrs. Rawlings' most frequent men visitors were her fiance Mr. Norton Baskin and his friends Bob Camp and Cecil Clark.

Mrs. Rawlings had what I would call two good women friends, Miss Dessie Smith and Miss Zelma Cason. I call them good friends because they would come in the house without being announced, and would order me to fix them something just as Mrs. Rawlings would. So far as I know, Miss Dessie and Miss Zelma were not friends with each other, for they never came together to Cross Creek.

Miss Dessie came often in her car. She was the one who taught Mrs. Rawlings how to fish and hunt and grow a vegetable garden. She also taught her to identify the different trees, plants, and wildlife around Cross Creek. Miss Dessie used to call Mrs. Rawlings "young-un," because when Mrs. Rawlings first came to Florida from Rochester she didn't know how to survive in the country, and Miss Dessie had to teach her. Many times Miss Dessie and Mrs. Rawlings would go on fishing trips for days. But I would still say that most of Mrs. Rawlings' fishing and hunting trips were with men. Mrs. Rawlings told me about the time Miss Dessie wanted her to join the WAC during World War II. When Mrs. Rawlings told her she couldn't leave Idella and Moe (the dog), Miss Dessie suggested that Idella join the colored WAC (Women's Army Corps) and that Moe could come along as a WAC mascot! As time went on, Miss Dessie didn't visit as often. Miss Dessie recently explained it to me this way: "She [Mrs. Rawlings] got too big for her britches; she didn't have time for me."

Miss Zelma lived in Citra, a few miles south of Island Grove on SR 301. She was at Cross Creek much more often than Miss Dessie was. Miss Zelma and Mrs. Rawlings rode on horseback together, taking the census, an event that helped Mrs. Rawlings gather material for her stories. Her good friend later became her enemy, however, when Zelma took offense at Mrs. Rawlings' description of her in her book *Cross Creek*. Miss Zelma sued Mrs. Rawlings for invasion of privacy. After an appeal reversing the decision of the lower court, she won the case, and while the judgment was only one dollar, it cost Mrs. Rawlings a lot more in time and legal expenses. Mrs. Rawlings never got over it, not because of the money as much as the betrayal of friendship.

It was several months after I came to Cross Creek that Mrs. Rawlings began to take me with her when she went to her cottage in Crescent Beach. The Crescent Beach house had been bought with some of the royalties from Mrs. Rawlings' first book. The house was (and still is) located just off the corner of U.S. Highway A1A and State Road 206. You turn off A1A on Jellison Avenue, a dirt road, and go one short block to the corner of Broward Avenue, another sandy road. The driveway led in through a thick growth of palmettos to the garage below the cottage. Winding steps, with a landing halfway up, led from the driveway to the cottage. You would enter the cottage's tiny kitchen. There was a window between the kitchen and the living room that you could pass things through. There was no dining room; Mrs. Rawlings had a small, drop-leaf table in the living room that she ate and typed on. The living room was painted a deep orchid color, for Mrs. Rawlings liked purple. A narrow hallway led from the kitchen toward the living room in one direction, and Mrs. Rawlings' bedroom in the other. One bedroom was straight across from that door, and the bathroom and other bedroom were down the hall. A door out the front opened to stairs that led down through the dunes to the ocean. That was all that was there at the time.

At the Cross Creek house, Mrs. Rawlings would announce at the spur of the moment that we were going to Crescent Beach, and I would have to get our things together in a hurry. It might be for just a day or weekend, or sometimes for weeks at a time.

Mrs. Rawlings' Crescent Beach house as it appeared in 1939, showing the steps leading up to the cottage from the driveway. Photo courtesy of the Marjorie Kinnan Rawlings Collection, Department of Special Collections, George A. Smathers Libraries, University of Florida.

Snakes. So many snakes. That's one of the things I remember most vividly about Crescent Beach. The cottage was set high atop a dune and was surrounded by thick palmettos all the way down to A1A. I stayed in a fixed-up room in the garage below the dune. My room had a little daybed, a chair, a table, and a lamp. There was a bathroom with a shower, which was high living for me compared to the tenant house at Cross Creek. The garage building was also surrounded by palmettos. And in those palmettos lived the longest, fattest rattlesnakes you can imagine.

One of my jobs was to get the mail from the mailbox located at the end of the road on A1A. Mrs. Rawlings told me to always drive the car when getting the mail, because of the rattlesnakes. She also said, "Don't ever try to run over big rattlesnakes; it'll turn the car over." I don't know why she told me that, but I wasn't taking any chances; I believed her. So there I'd be, driving ever so carefully down the sandy road to the mailbox, and a rattlesnake would be in my way. I kept the windows rolled up tight, for I was scared, and I would sit there in that broiling summer heat waiting for the rattlesnake to oh so slowly slither off into the brush. Of course, there was no such thing as air-conditioning in cars in those days, so you know how suffering hot it was.

In my place in the garage, there was a small square window in the bathroom that I kept open to catch the sea breezes at night. Each night I would hear a strange crackling noise under that window. I asked Leonard, Mrs. Rawlings' yardman at Crescent Beach, what it could be. He said, "Ah, that's nothing but an ol' rattlesnake." I can tell you, I never opened that window again, sea breeze or not. Every night I was terrified, as I had to walk down the narrow steps in the dark, through the palmettos that led from the cottage to the driveway below, to get to my room. Why I never stepped on a rattlesnake I don't know.

One morning at the cottage, I spotted a snake directly under the head of Mrs. Rawlings' bed. I don't know what kind of snake it was, but it wasn't a rattlesnake. Mrs. Rawlings jumped right out of bed and killed it with a poker. I never did get used to the snakes.

I remember the day Mrs. Rawlings lost her beloved dog, Pat. It was near Christmas in 1941. We were coming over to Cross Creek from Crescent Beach, me to go home to Reddick and Mrs. Rawlings to deliver her Christmas cheer to the Cross Creek neighbors. Mrs. Rawlings told me I could take the car as soon as I completed unpacking and putting things in order for her at the house. Pat, her black-and-white bird dog, was so happy to be

Marjorie Kinnan Rawlings at Cross Creek with her dog Pat. The dog was struck and killed by a car in front of the property just before Christmas 1941. Photo courtesy of the Marjorie Kinnan Rawlings Collection, Department of Special Collections, George A. Smathers Libraries, University of Florida.

home and not closed up in the cottage that he went running out of the yard. He jumped over the cattle guard right in the path of a passing car. He was killed instantly. You would have thought it was Mrs. Rawlings or I who had been killed, to hear the screaming and yelling so loud. All the Mickenses, most of the neighbors, and the man who was driving the car came running to see what could be done. We were hugging each other and could not stop crying. Oh, it was a sad time for us at the Creek. I did not go home that night. The next day Pat was buried under the magnolia tree on the west side of the house. I went home to Reddick after the burial.

I don't know if Mrs. Rawlings bought her next bird dog, Moe, or if someone gave Moe to her, but it was done in a hurry. Moe was white with brown spots. He grew very fast and tried hard to take Pat's place in our lives.

After about three or four months of my stay at Cross Creek, Mrs. Rawlings bought me a nice bedroom set. This was certainly an improvement in my living conditions, and I appreciated it. Then, in 1941, she had a small apartment added to the back of the tenant house for me. This gave us all a lot more space, and it was a lovely change, although short lived, for she and Mr. Baskin were married in October of 1941, and not long after that the three of us moved to St. Augustine.

After she and Mr. Baskin married, we divided our time between his hotel in St. Augustine and the Crescent Beach house, with less and less time spent at Cross Creek.

CHAPTER 6 »

Nobody Knows the Trouble I've Seen

M RS. RAWLINGS' troubles didn't start when she married Mr. Baskin or when we moved to St. Augustine; they had been there all along. Gradually, though, as the years went by, the troubles compounded and got worse. And it didn't take long for her troubles to cause me to have troubles too.

When I first started working for Mrs. Rawlings, I didn't know how much she drank. Each day she would work at the table with her typewriter. On her left was a big glass ashtray that would always be full by the end of the day, as I've mentioned earlier. In front of her was a vase of fresh-cut flowers. On the right-hand side of her typewriter was a brown paper bag. It was awhile before I realized that she had an open flask of whiskey in that bag, and she drank from it liberally while she worked. Even then, I never saw how much the level of whiskey went down in the flask or how many times she may have refilled it from the supply in her liquor cabinet.

Marjorie Rawlings and Norton Baskin were married in St. Augustine on October 27, 1941. Photo courtesy of the Marjorie Kinnan Rawlings Collection, Department of Special Collections, George A. Smathers Libraries, University of Florida.

Each day Mrs. Rawlings would work at her typewriter. On one side was a big ashtray, in front of her a vase of fresh-cut flowers, and on the other side a brown paper bag containing a flask of whiskey. Photo by Erich Hartmann, used at the Marjorie Kinnan Rawlings Collection, Department of Special Collections, George A. Smathers Libraries, University of Florida.

As the months went by, I came to recognize the signs that she was drinking too much. Her behavior began to change; she would become upset at the least little thing and yell. I was the one she usually yelled at, because I was the closest at hand. I would get angry at the unfairness of being made the target of her frustrations. I could tell by the redness of her face and her facial expressions when the whiskey was affecting her. Many times she would say, "No, I'm not going to have any lunch," and I'd know then that she'd had too much. Her mood might change without warning. There would be periods of depression, and she would cry. Or she might become belligerent, insisting that she was going to drive when I knew she was drunk.

Most of the time, Mrs. Rawlings was content to let me do the driving whenever we went somewhere together. This was fine with me, because in my opinion Mrs. Rawlings always drove too fast, and I sure didn't want to ride with her after she'd been drinking all morning. But that's the very time Mrs. Rawlings would decide she wanted to drive. More than once, we had a struggle over the keys. She would exclaim, "I can drive! I'm not drunk. I want to drive, get out of my way."

And I would argue, "No, Mrs. Rawlings, I'll drive."

Sometimes she would give up disgustedly and let me drive, and sometimes she won. Then she would drive way too fast, because she was mad.

More than once after she acted that way toward me, I would tell myself I'd had enough. I wasn't going to work for her anymore if she was going to treat me that way. I would have Mrs. Rawlings drop me off at Mama's in Reddick for what she would think was a visit, with the understanding that I would catch a ride back to Cross Creek. Then I would determine not to go back and just not bother catching that ride. Those were the times she would realize she had treated me badly, and she would come looking for me, all apologies and, promising it wouldn't happen again. I believed her in the beginning, and I went back knowing she needed me. Each time she would give me money, and because she knew I liked new clothes, she would tell me to go buy a new dress or something. That was her way of trying to appease me. Mama grew to hate her for the way she treated me, saying, "I don't know why you keep going back to that woman."

One of those times must have been in April of 1942, for Mrs. Rawlings lamented in a letter to Mr. Baskin in St. Augustine that I had not come home yet, and she wondered, "What the hell if anything of the sort has happened to Idella." Later in the same letter, she wrote, "The Idella situation has me depressed . . ."[1] In another letter written in July of the same year, she wrote to a friend that I was on vacation and that she had a "tongue-tied darky" working for her as a substitute.[2] Now Mrs. Rawlings never gave me a vacation, so I'm sure that that's how she decided to explain my absence to her friends.

Once Mrs. Rawlings and Mr. Baskin had settled into their new penthouse apartment at the top of his Castle Warden Hotel, Mrs. Rawlings needed to find a place for me to stay. She took me to the colored section of town and paid for a room for me in a boarding-house. She let me keep the car so I could drive back and forth from the boardinghouse to the hotel. Whenever I visited friends at the Florida Normal College campus, they thought the car was mine, and I didn't tell them otherwise. Once one of them said, "Idella, didn't I see a white lady driving your car the other day?"

I just said, "Oh, yeah, I let her drive it sometimes."

Mrs. Rawlings and Mr. Baskin had two good friends in St. Augustine, Verle and Edith Pope. Mr. Pope became a state senator in 1948. The four of them were very close. In terms of friendship, I would say that Edith Pope was to Mrs. Rawlings in St. Augustine what Dessie was to Mrs. Rawlings in Cross Creek. Once Edith Pope came over to the house in Cross Creek for an overnight visit. She got up early in the morning and went walking outside on the grass

The boardinghouse where Mrs. Rawlings rented a room for Idella when they moved to St. Augustine.

and saw a snake. It was a coral snake, but she didn't know it when she yelled, "Oh, such a pretty snake!" She talked with what I guess was an English accent, exclaiming, "Margie, look at this snake."

When Mrs. Rawlings saw what she was looking at, she yelled, "Ooh, that's a coral. Don't move! Don't move!" She got her gun and shot the snake. Then she said to Mrs. Pope, "I guess you better go home."

It didn't take long for Mrs. Rawlings to get restless in St. Augustine. While it suited Mr. Baskin just right, hotel life was not for her. I could tell that she was torn between her desire to be with him and her need to be alone so she could write. We would go to Crescent Beach to stay so she could have that solitude, but then she would get lonely, missing Mr. Baskin, and want him to come down. She expected him to come whenever she called for him, but he couldn't always do that because of his business. He was needed at the hotel. Sometimes he would say he was coming for the weekend, and she would happily send me away with the car, giving me the time off. Then when I got back she would be very depressed, because something had come up and Mr. Baskin had not been able to make it after all. Other times he would come and she would act like she didn't want him around because he was getting in the way of her trying to write. They had many arguments about that, and they are reflected in some of her letters.

It was while staying in Crescent Beach that I met the man who would eventually become my first husband—Bernard Young. Crescent Beach was about two miles south of Butler's Beach, for many years the only area beach for blacks. It was named for its developer, Frank B. Butler, who started a real estate business in 1925 and bought up land along that stretch of the ocean in order to establish a beach for blacks. He sold lots along the beach, where blacks built houses and set up various businesses.[3] Whenever they could get away, those blacks who were able to came down from St. Augustine to the beach.

I had never heard of Butler's Beach, so I didn't know it was there, but after the day I met Bernard I often enjoyed going when I had time off. I later made friends with Pinkie Horne, who managed a hamburger concession stand. That made my life at Crescent Beach better, for I had some friends and would walk or drive down to the beach whenever I could.

The day I met Bernard was a Wednesday afternoon. I had completed my work in the cottage and called Mrs. Rawlings' bird dog, as I often did, to go for a walk along the edge of the ocean. The dog loved to swim in the surf and run along the beach, and I enjoyed the company, for it was lonely wherever I lived with Mrs. Rawlings. As we started walking, I saw some small dots moving way off in the distance. I said, "Come on, Moe. Let's go see who those people are." We ran some, and walked some, and when we finally got to Butler's Beach the people were far out in the ocean,

A historical plaque in Idella's honor was placed on this house at 81 Kings Ferry Way in St. Augustine after the 1998 Marjorie Kinnan Rawlings Convention. It was Bernard's mother's house, where Idella lived after she married Bernard.

swimming. They came ashore, two men shaking themselves. They asked me who I was and where I came from. After telling them the story of my job, I think they felt sorry for me. They were from St. Augustine. One said he owned the ice-cream stand at the drug store; the other was Bernard, who said he was at the barbershop on the same street.

They both told me to come by if I was ever in town.

It did not take me long to ask Mrs. Rawlings if I could take the car and drive into town. Oh, I was happy to have something to do each Wednesday, other than work, read, or sleep.

Bernard and I became a twosome, and we had many happy times playing cards with friends at his mother's house, where he lived with his two small children from a former marriage, Beasie and Charlie. One such night I became very sick. Bernard's mother, Johnney, called Mrs. Rawlings, and Mrs. Rawlings instructed them to take me to the hospital; she would meet us there. She told Bernard to bring the car so she could have it to go home in.

They drove me to Flagler Hospital in spite of my protests, and it's a good thing they did, because I had appendicitis. In those days blacks and whites were put in separate wings of the hospital, so after the operation to remove my appendix I was given a room in the "colored" wing. Mrs. Rawlings came to visit me often, any time of day or night, whenever she felt like it. Once I heard her arguing with the nurse; it was late at night, after visiting hours, and the nurse didn't want to let her in. Mrs. Rawlings could be very assertive when she wanted to, and she usually wanted to after a few drinks. I heard her tell the nurse, "That's my girl. I'll visit her anytime I want to." And she got her way. From then on I would know when she was coming because I would hear the loud clackity-clack of her shoes as she walked down the long hallway, and the nurses would tease me, saying, "Here comes your mama."

Flagler Hospital, where Idella was taken when she had appendicitis. Mrs. Rawlings visited her here and paid all her medical expenses.

I must have gotten an infection or something after the operation, because my recovery did not go well. Once when I was in and out of sleep, I heard the doctors talking about sending for my sister from Florida Normal College. I needed another operation, and they were looking for blood donors whose blood matched mine.

The next thing I knew, all my family was there, but only my sister Eliza and a friend from college had blood that matched mine. At about the same time they were giving blood, in strode Mrs. Rawlings, obviously tipsy. When she understood what was going on, she insisted they test her blood too. Lo and behold, Mrs. Rawlings' blood was the same type as mine. Mama (my real one) was fit to be tied. "You are *not* putting that woman's blood in my baby," she told the doctors. "It's nothing but whiskey in her veins."

The doctors took Mama aside and persuaded her that the blood was needed. After that I began to get better. Mrs. Rawlings continued to visit me any time she wished. She looked worse and worse each time she came, dressed in any old thing, her hair unkempt. She kept telling me to hurry and get well because she needed me. I could tell by looking at her that she was right. By this time I could have finished recuperating at home, but Mrs. Rawlings had to go to New York, and she insisted, even telling the doctors that I stay in the hospital until I was well enough to return to work. She paid for the entire stay, which was about six weeks in all.

Things did not get better with Mrs. Rawlings after I returned to work. Her bouts of depression, frustration and anger came more and more frequently, all the while accompanied by heavy drinking. Again I felt I couldn't take it anymore, and that I had to leave.

I had a friend from Reddick, Luverne, who had moved to New York and had a good paying job on Long Island, working for some rich white folks. My cousin Lillie Wilson had also given up her teaching job in Broward County and had gone to New York to find a job. Lillie kept trying to get Thelma and me to come up there and work. This was around June of 1943. It was during the war. Lillie said things were good and work was not hard to find. Thelma had just finished school and was eager to go, and I decided it was a good time for me to get away from Mrs. Rawlings, somewhere where she couldn't come and find me and persuade me to come back.

So Thelma and I traveled to the big city of New York. Just getting off the train at Penn Station—that was something. I was amazed at the size of the place and the number of people going this way and that. Later, had I known how to get back to that train station, I would have, and gone back home too. I didn't appreciate New York; I didn't like what I saw. Thelma and I stayed with Lil at first, and I remember the constant noise, flashing lights, the sounds of traffic and people talking and shouting all night long. It wasn't what I thought it was going to be, and it wasn't anything like I was accustomed to in Reddick or Cross Creek. Even little things like breakfast were not the same. Now it's a habit I still have: I get my breakfast, I don't care where I am. But at Lil's—no breakfast! They didn't have anything for breakfast. They were smoking all the time; I guess it was just their type of living, but it wasn't for me. I stayed, since I couldn't get back to Penn Station, and I had to accept what I couldn't change. It was exciting after I got over my fear of being there.

Lillie got us a room in Harlem at the home of an old lady who was a friend of hers, and Luverne found me a job with a nice Jamaican family on Long Island, the Richardses. I rode on a subway for the first time to make the trip to Long Island. I carried with me my signed copy of *Cross Creek Cookery* as proof that I had cooked for the famous author Marjorie Kinnan Rawlings. I used as many of the recipes from that book as I could, but found that the Richardses weren't used to southern dishes and liked their

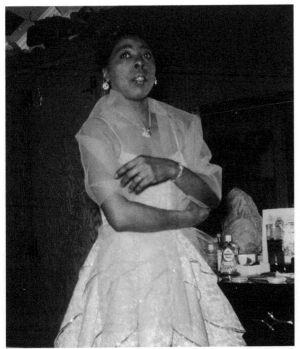

Idella's cousin Lillie in their room in New York City. Idella went there to "escape" from Mrs. Rawlings and got a job cooking for a couple on Long Island.

food cooked differently. I was really stumped the first time they asked me to cook broiled liver. Mrs. Richards told me not to cook it too much, just medium rare. I had never fixed liver in Cross Creek, and there was no broiler in the wood stove I cooked on there, so I could only guess how to do it. I ran it under the broiler just long enough for it to look done enough to me. After I served it, Mrs. Richards was furious. She stormed into the kitchen, fussing, "This liver is raw! Just what kind of food did you people eat at that Creek?"

I did just what an obedient colored worker was supposed to do in those days: I buttoned my lip and kept my reply to myself. But I had a chance for a comeback a little while later. Mrs. Richards needed to bring something to a fancy luncheon her club was having at the Waldorf Astoria in New York City. She asked me for ideas, and I suggested a nice ham. I told her what to buy, and I prepared the ham the way Mrs. Rawlings had taught me in Cross Creek. After the ham was decorated with cloves, pineapple slices and cherries, it was beautiful. Mrs. Richards exclaimed over it and told me about all the compliments she had received. I told her, "That's one of the things we people ate at Cross Creek."

The room Thelma and I stayed in was just two blocks from the Apollo Theater. That was one of the biggest places for black entertainment, and we went there often to see plays and other events. It was a good place to go after work or on my day off. One day I went there alone. I stayed through one show after another. When I left it was dark. I hadn't realized it while I was inside the theater, because I couldn't see outside. Coming out, the exit was on a different side of the building than where I went in, and my head was all turned around. My house was right around the corner, but I was lost. So I hailed a taxicab to take me home. The driver turned around and asked, "Where to?" I told him, and he shook his head and said he wasn't going to take me there; the house was right up the street. Looking back, that was really good for that man to tell me that, for in New York unsuspecting people were and are taken advantage of all the time. He could surely have taken advantage of my ignorance that day.

I had been working for the Richards family only about six weeks when I heard from Mrs. Rawlings. How she found out where I was or got my address, I have never found out, but one day when I returned to my room in Harlem there was a letter from her waiting for me. She was in New York at the Harkness Hospital, suffering from bronchial flu and an attack of diverticulitis. Mr. Baskin had just left for the service a few days before; he was to be an ambulance driver for the American Field Service. In her letter, Mrs. Rawlings asked me to telephone her at the hospital, and she gave the date she would be leaving it.

I always did as I was told, so I did call, but I waited for three days after the date she gave me, sure she would already be gone. There was no phone in my room, but there was a pay phone down the hall, and that's what I used to place the call. Just my luck, she was still there.

We had a very tearful conversation, and somehow she convinced me to visit her at the hospital. When I went she talked and talked, pleaded and persuaded, and finally I agreed to try again with her after I came home to Reddick for Christmas. She gave me money to pay for the fare home, and agreed to pay me a much higher salary when I returned. I had been making thirty-five dollars a week with the Richardses, whereas the last time I worked for Mrs. Rawlings I was only up to five dollars a week.

The beginning of a northern winter was another first for me. It was real exciting to see the snow for the first time, but the cold was awful. Ice was something I hadn't reckoned with before. Getting off the subway on Long Island, you had to go up the steps to a landing and then down some steps to the street again. One cold morning, the steps were covered with ice. I did all right getting up the steps, but starting down, I slipped. I yelled to the people below, "I'm coming! I'm coming!" as I went sliding down those steps. I said to myself, Uh uh, I'm going home. You can't hardly walk.

Mama was happy to hear we were coming back. She had been writing us all along, telling us to come home. Thelma never did work while we were in New York; she was looking for a job the whole time we were there. Mama wanted her to come home and start teaching. So Thelma and I went home to Reddick at Christmastime, and after that I went back to work for Mrs. Rawlings.

Early in 1944, a short time after I returned to Mrs. Rawlings, she surprised me by asking me if there was anything I wanted to do in my life. She said, "Idella, I don't want you to ever have to work for another white woman. I mean that." I often wonder if

Mrs. Rawlings said this because I had worked in New York and told her how nice those people were. We were in the car on the way to Crescent Beach, and I didn't answer right away. Finally I told her that I had always wanted to go to cosmetology school and learn how to do ladies' hair. So Mrs. Rawlings arranged for me to go to Apex Beauty College in Atlanta, Georgia, paying my tuition and other expenses. She arranged for me to take extra lessons at night to learn how to fix white ladies' hair, so I could do her hair for her when I returned. While I was there I heard of a better beauty school in Tampa, Angelo Beauty School, where a friend of mine was going. So I transferred and finished the course there. It took about nine months in all to complete the course.

Then it was back to Mrs. Rawlings, back to her constant, restless moving back and forth between Crescent Beach and Cross Creek. Things were worse than they ever were before. By this time, Mrs. Rawlings had received word that Mr. Baskin was sick—suffering from amoebic dysentery—in India where he was stationed. She now had that worry, compounded with the invasion-of-privacy lawsuit that Miss Zelma Cason was bringing against her because of the portrayal in *Cross Creek*. She had also begun work on *The Sojourner* and felt that the writing was going badly.[4] She was drinking constantly, and was cranky as all-get-out. All of these problems made it very difficult for me to deal with her every day. It was impossible to reason with her, and soon I couldn't stand it anymore. I made plans to leave her again.

This time, I went to Jacksonville and lived with Hettie. I soon found a job working in a photography darkroom. After two weeks of training, I had a sudden compulsive urge to go home to Mama. I can't explain it, but I just knew I had to go.

I woke Hettie up that morning and told her, "I'm going home today."

Hettie said, "I thought you were going to work."

"I'll have to call them," I said. "I have to get home."

I was in a hurry and had Hettie take me to the bus station. I took the bus to Reddick, where it let me off on 441, next to the white children's school. From there I walked home to Mama's. Mama was surprised to see me but glad just the same. Papa and Dorothy had both gone to work. Later that morning, Mama went out to the sweet-potato patch to work. The sweet-potato patch was north of the house, at the back of the property near the barn. I stayed behind at the house. A little while later, I saw Mr. Davis from the telegraph office coming up the driveway. When he got to the house, I could tell by the look on his face that something was terribly wrong. During wartime, the last person you want to see coming to your door is the telegraph deliveryman. Mr. Davis held out the telegram and said, "Give this to Ethel. I'm sorry."

The telegraph said that my brother E. M. was missing, but it gave no other details. I wasn't even sure what it meant, and I didn't want to believe it. I couldn't bear to show it to Mama, so I folded it and put it in my pocket. I carried around both the telegram and a gut-wrenching pain all afternoon until Dorothy came home. Mama had come to the house and gone back to the potato patch, but I hadn't said a word to her about it. When Dorothy got there I took her to the outhouse where Mama wouldn't see us, and showed her the telegram. We sat in that little outhouse and cried and cried, hugging each other for the longest time. Finally we talked about what we should do. We had to tell Mama, and I was appointed the one to do it.

Mama was still in the garden cleaning out the sweet potatoes. I walked out there and stooped down with the telegraph in my hand. I said, "Mama, what does it mean when they say someone is missing?"

She looked up, and seeing the telegram in my hand, exclaimed, "What? E. M. is missing?" She dropped her hoe and reached for the telegram. "Let me see that."

The classification of missing is worse, I think, than the

notification of killed in action, at least when the outcome is ultimately the same. It was almost a year before the service finally sent E. M.'s things, including his dog tags, and told us that he was presumed killed. That year was spent in uncertainty, fearing to hope that he might somehow still be alive.

The last correspondence we had received from E. M. was a Mother's Day card he had sent to Mama. I still have that card. In it he wrote: "I hope that you are in the best of health this wonderful day. And may you live to see many more. I hope to spend the

Idella's brother, E. M., visiting at Hettie's in Jacksonville while on leave from the Army. He and Sadie were married just before he was sent overseas.

Papa with Joyce Ann, E. M.'s daughter. Sadie was good about letting Mama and Papa see Joyce Ann.

next one with you (smiles). Give my best to the family and friends. I remain your son, E. M."

My last two letters to E. M. were dated November 7 and November 13, 1944. He never received them, and they were returned to me, stamped MISSING in bold letters, one in February and one in March of 1945. In the letters I told E. M. about his baby girl, Joyce Ann. He had named her, but he never got to see her. This was Mama and Papa's first grandchild, and she became very special to us all. E. M.'s wife, Sadie, was good about letting Mama and Papa keep Joyce Ann whenever they wanted, which turned out to be almost every weekend.

It was the waiting and worrying that was so hard. I developed stomach ulcers and was told to go on a special, strict diet for a year. In the meantime, I heard from Mrs. Rawlings again. She was in New York, staying with Mr. Baskin, who had been sent home from India and was being treated for his dysentery at the hospital there. Once again, she used her gift with words to convince me to go to Cross Creek ahead of them and prepare the house for Mr. Baskin's convalescence.[5]

By the end of April 1945, Mr. Baskin was well enough to take back management of the hotel. Mrs. Rawlings and I went to the cottage in Crescent Beach. She was doing very little writing, mostly just letters, it seemed. Mr. Baskin came to the cottage infrequently, sometimes only one evening a week, which upset her. There were obvious tensions between them when they were together. I never heard them really arguing loudly, but I could tell when they were mad at each other. I would carry lunch or something in, and one would be in one corner of the room and one in the other. Mrs. Rawlings would be reading and Mr. Baskin would be holding a book and pretending to read, I guess. There would be nothing but silence; not a word between them would I hear.

Sometimes Mrs. Rawlings would say to me, "Let's go!" and we'd up and leave in a hurry. Mr. Baskin wouldn't know half the time where we were. She would just go without saying a word to him.

We were back and forth between the cottage and Cross Creek that summer. Mr. Baskin came even less often to Cross Creek, partially because gas rationing was still in effect. Mrs. Rawlings tried hard to find a balance between her duties to her marriage and her need to be alone to write. She tried to please him, and she tried to please herself. In the fall Mrs. Rawlings had some work done to the cottage to turn it into a year-round residence, so she could be closer to Mr. Baskin. The fireplace was added to the cottage, and at the same time she enlarged my space in the garage,

When Mrs. Rawlings was drinking heavily, she became depressed and no longer seemed to care about her appearance. Her hair wasn't neat, and Idella would have to urge her to put on a clean dress. Photo by Erich Hartmann, used at the Marjorie Kinnan Rawlings Collection, Department of Special Collections, George A. Smathers Libraries, University of Florida.

which she referred to as the maid's quarters.[6] My "new" quarters included a living room with a couch that converted to a bed for guests. She also bought me a new bedroom set for my bedroom, as I mentioned earlier.

Most of Mrs. Rawlings' energies that winter were devoted to her upcoming trial. Her writing, by her own accounts, was put practically on hold until the trial was over. Her moods varied from upbeat and optimistic to dark despair, with little warning of the impending shift.

Meanwhile, I had resumed my relationship with Bernard. He kept wanting me to leave "that old woman" and go with him. He was handsome and charming, and I was in love. He said he would take care of me so I wouldn't have to work anymore. His promises sounded wonderful to me. I took him home to Reddick to introduce him to Mama and the rest of the family. I was proud to show off this wonderful man I had found, and I was not prepared for Mama's reaction. To put it mildly, she was not impressed. She called me into the kitchen and said, "Della, that man is no good. Let him alone." I thought Mama was being very unfair to judge Bernard like that, without getting to know him the way I thought I did. I was mad and embarrassed to have brought him home, and we left shortly after that. That was one time—perhaps I should have—but I didn't obey Mama and stop seeing Bernard. Mama did take the wind from my sails, however, and I didn't quit my job and run away with him right away, either.

When the outcome of the lawsuit filed by Miss Cason was decided in Mrs. Rawlings' favor in May of 1946, she was relieved. Finally she was sure that that summer she could get back to her serious writing. But the trial left her exhausted as well. After a brief period of elation, the months of worry and tension caught up with her. She went through the motions, but her moods were as volatile as ever. Finally, early in 1947, she decided to move back to Cross Creek to stay until she could begin to make some progress on her writing.[7] Meanwhile, Miss Zelma had filed an appeal.

By this time, it was plain to me that Mrs. Rawlings had a drinking problem, but I was powerless to help her. Once, when I said something, she told me that the whiskey helped her memory and she could get more work done when she drank. She started to look bad and no longer seemed to care about her appearance. I would have to urge her to put on a clean dress when we were going to town. Sometimes I was ashamed of her because of the way she acted.

Then in April, something happened that changed the course of our relationship again. I was supposed to go home to Reddick, but when I reminded Mrs. Rawlings about it, she had forgotten. She started yelling and cussing at me. "Why do you always have to be going to Reddick?" She carried on, until finally I told her I was

Idella would serve Mrs. Rawlings tea in the living room of the Crescent Beach cottage. Her dog Moe and Idella were often her only companions, as Mr. Baskin's hotel work and the obvious tensions between the couple kept him away for long periods. Photo courtesy of the Marjorie Kinnan Rawlings Collection, Department of Special Collections, George A. Smathers Libraries, University of Florida.

sick and wanted to go home. She grabbed the keys and stomped out, hollering for me to "Come on, then."

It was raining, and we didn't know that the road department had recently oiled the road. That, along with the whiskey and anger-fed recklessness with which she was driving, made a dangerous combination. Rounding a bend with way too much speed, the car skidded and went off the road, hitting a fence. The car rolled over twice, coming to rest on its side. It's a miracle we weren't both killed. Mrs. Rawlings always gave credit to her sturdy Oldsmobiles whenever she had a wreck, which was often. Each time she smashed up a car, she bought another Olds. I gave the credit to God that I wasn't killed. Mrs. Rawlings got by that time with some pretty severe scrapes and bruises, but I was in a lot of pain, with two broken ribs.

Mrs. Rawlings had Little Will drive me in the truck to Dr. Strange in McIntosh. He patched up my ribs but told me I was just an inch or so from being paralyzed. "You stay with Marge long enough," he warned me, "and she'll kill you yet."

A few days after the accident, Mrs. Rawlings came to Reddick to check on me. Mama was livid about it. She had been fussing ever since the accident, saying, "I told you so." She didn't want to let Mrs. Rawlings in, but Mrs. Rawlings could be even more assertive than Mama could be. She just walked right in anyway.

The second time Mrs. Rawlings came to see me, Mama tried to stop her again. This time she not only came in, she exclaimed over Mama's white beans and ham she smelled cooking on the stove in the kitchen. Mrs. Rawlings, without even asking, helped herself to a bowl, sitting right down at Mama's dining room table! Mama couldn't get over the nerve of that woman.

I didn't realize the meaning of it then, but thinking back, I do believe that Mama was as prejudiced about whites as some whites were about blacks. I remember that whenever a white insurance man came to the door, Mama always made him stand out on the

Idella's first husband, Bernard Young, whom she met at Butler's Beach while staying at Crescent Beach with Mrs. Rawlings.

porch while she went to get her payment. It didn't matter if it was cold or rainy; she didn't want a white man in her house.

I recuperated at home for several weeks, all the while listening to Mama's admonitions about Mrs. Rawlings. When it was time to go back to work with her, I got to thinking about what Dr. Strange had said to me. Bernard's sweet talk—and the promise that I wouldn't ever have to work for "that old woman" anymore, that he would take care of me—sounded better all the time. Within a few weeks Bernard and I made the decision to get married. I was to move in with him at his mother's house in St. Augustine. I didn't dare tell Mrs. Rawlings that I was going to get married, boy no! There was no fancy wedding; we just went to a judge's office and got married. Bernard took two of his friends with him as witnesses. It was only afterwards and with great fear that I told Mrs. Rawlings that I wouldn't be working for her anymore. She was very upset. "Idella, you *can't* leave me," she cried.

But I was determined not to be dissuaded, and in the end she wished me well. Shortly after our marriage, Mrs. Rawlings left to spend the summer in Van Hornesville, New York. Mr. and Mrs.

Owen Young had offered to let her use their summer home to work on her novel *The Sojourner.* The countryside in Van Hornesville was similar to the setting of the novel, but I think the Youngs knew she just needed to get away for awhile, where she could write in peace. Mrs. Rawlings so liked it there that she bought an old farmhouse and set about having it renovated so she could use it the following summer. Mr. Baskin had the cottage in Crescent Beach enlarged for her while she was in New York, hoping, I'm sure, that the improvements would make her content to stay there longer. That August she wrote this about me while she was in Van Hornesville:

> I have done nothing about maid's quarters. [Referring to the renovations underway in the farmhouse she bought,] Idella up and got married this spring, after I went on paying her regular wages while she recovered from our automobile accident. I had also bought an expensive combination bed-davenport for her new suite in the tenant house at Cross Creek, so she could have a guest. And she had known for months she was going to leave. Now her husband is in an Army hospital with stomach ulcers, Idella is lost without her own money, and not at all happy. We may possibly get together for the winter.[8]

It was true that after just a few weeks of being married to Bernard, I was not happy. Bernard didn't turn out to be the husband I anticipated. He didn't have any ambition to work and get ahead, and we had a very volatile relationship. It was most apparent that I wouldn't be able to depend on Bernard to "take care of me," so it wasn't long before I was ready to go back to Mrs. Rawlings. It seemed the lesser of two evils. When Mrs. Rawlings came back from Van Hornesville, she came to see me. She came over to Johnny's (Bernard's mother's house, where we were staying), and tooted her horn. I went out, and she said, "Idella, now you know

Mrs. Rawlings and Moe on the porch of the house she bought in Van Hornesville, New York. Idella started spending summers here with Mrs. Rawlings in 1948. Photo courtesy of the Marjorie Kinnan Rawlings Collection, Department of Special Collections, George A. Smathers Libraries, University of Florida.

I need you. I know what I'm going to do. Bernard can get a job there with Norton and the two of you can stay in the suite at the cottage." So that November I returned to Mrs. Rawlings, and Mr. Baskin gave Bernard a job at the bar at Marineland, for by this time he had taken over the franchise of the Dolphin Restaurant there. Bernard and I both moved into the garage apartment at Crescent Beach. His two children continued to live with Johnnie or with their mother, Dorothy. This arrangement didn't last long, for Bernard was lazy and irresponsible. One of his jobs was to pick up workers from St. Augustine in one of Mr. Baskin's jeeps and drive them to the restaurant. Then he worked in the bar, and that was the wrong place, I imagine, for he kept wrecking those jeeps. Finally Mr. Baskin had to fire him. Bernard was angry and tried hard to get me to quit my job too. We had a big fight, but I refused to quit, knowing one of us had to work. Eventually Bernard went back to barbering in St. Augustine.

The next year, 1948, Mrs. Rawlings and I began to spend summers in Van Hornesville, New York. We would take turns driving, with the dog and cat in the back seat. I remember once when it was my turn to drive, Mrs. Rawlings spotted a semi-truck in front of us. It had several license plates on the back, as such trucks do, and Mrs. Rawlings must have seen a New York plate. She told me, "Idella, keep up with that truck; he'll take us right to New York." So, fast or slow, I stayed behind that truck. If it stopped, we stopped. When the truck finally stopped for good, or when Mrs. Rawlings came to her senses, she found that we had followed that truck to Youngstown, Ohio. How she cursed me for following that truck.

"Why did you do it?" she demanded. "The map is right beside you. Now I've got to find some place for us to stay."

Finding a place to stay was no easy job in the days of segregation, because blacks were not allowed in the same places as whites. Also, most places didn't allow pets. Mrs. Rawlings took over the driving and finally pulled into a rundown-looking trailer court. The man there said that there was an old cabin out back that I could stay in. So Mrs. Rawlings paid the man and then snuck the animals in, hiding the cat under her sweater.

It was becoming more and more difficult for me to cope with Mrs. Rawlings' moods and unseemly behavior. I was afraid to ride with her because of her many accidents. She would apologize each time and promise it wouldn't happen again, but it always did.

In March of 1949, after Mr. Baskin sold the Castle Warden Hotel, Mrs. Rawlings had her lawyer from Jacksonville, Philip May, come to draw up a new will. She showed me the will when it was finished, because she wanted me to see that she had made provisions for me. She told me, "Idella, it says right here that if you're with me 'til I die, you'll receive fifty dollars a month as long as you live." She had made the same provision for Martha Mickens. She also told me that in that will, she left the cottage in Crescent Beach to Mr. Baskin. "And that's all," she said. I do believe she hoped that promise of fifty dollars a month would bind me to her and that I would not leave her again.

Mrs. Rawlings was well aware of the problems her drinking was causing in her life and in her marriage. She shared some of those feelings in a letter to Norman Berg, the representative of Macmillan in the Southeast, in February 1949. In it she wrote: "I may be fooling myself in thinking that the excessive drinking is the effect, and not the cause of my mental and emotional disturbance..." and "I think that he [Mr. Baskin] himself will be happier when I remove myself to a large degree. He said the other day that he could not take much more of my desperation. I have been punishing him as much as myself."[9]

I could tell that things were not going well with them, and I knew that they were sleeping in separate bedrooms at the cottage.

The summer of 1949 in Van Hornesville was the worst for me. Mrs. Rawlings was still beside herself with grief over the death of Max Perkins, her editor and friend. It had been two years since his death, but she still missed him terribly. She would pace back and forth, smoking and crying. When I asked her what was the matter, she would say, "Max is dead. What am I going to do?"

She had been very wrapped up in Max. She was always on the phone or exchanging letters with him. She really depended on him when she needed advice about her writing, and now he was gone.

Mrs. Rawlings drank constantly and heavily that summer. Her face was drawn and her eyes sunken. She didn't seem to care about her appearance. She was lonely and cried often. Once, she called Mr. Baskin and asked him to come up. I heard her say, "You've got to come *now*," and then "Why?" when he apparently said he couldn't. He came several days later, but as soon as he got there they had an argument. I could see them out the window coming down the hill, and I could tell by the way they walked that there was disputing between them.

Mr. Baskin said, "I can't just up and leave anytime you want me to. I have a business to attend to." He stayed just a few days.

She talked about suicidal thoughts in one of the letters she wrote that summer. She never expressed those thoughts to me, but I was worried about the possibility of it all the same.

I'll never forget the evening she came home after visiting and drinking with the Youngs all afternoon. On the spur of the moment she had invited them to dinner, and she asked me to cook a rib roast. Well, the roast was frozen. By the time I got it cooked, Mrs. Rawlings had put away several more drinks with her guests. Just as I was serving dinner, Mrs. Rawlings excused herself suddenly and went upstairs. I continued to serve the Youngs, and after a few moments we heard a loud thump upstairs. We all looked at each other, and I said, "Let me go up and see about her."

I opened the door to Mrs. Rawlings' room and found her sitting on the floor, without a stitch of clothes on. I tried to help her up, but she refused, pulling a sheet around her and saying she was all right. She admonished me not to tell anyone.

I went down and finished serving the guests, explaining that Mrs. Rawlings wasn't feeling well. But they knew, they knew as well as I did.

The next morning Mrs. Rawlings didn't remember much, but she remembered enough to ask me about it. I was tired of such scenes, and having to make excuses for her.

I took a few days off to visit friends in Brooklyn, and while I was there I got word that Papa Jake had died. I couldn't get back to Van Hornesville in time to get clothes and money to travel to Florida for the funeral, so I wired flowers and my apologies to the family for not being there.

Bernard did go, taking a bus from St. Augustine. He was upset that I wasn't there. I'm sure he figured I'd come, and he could convince me not to go back afterwards. He wrote me a letter telling me he was going to move to New York City and stay with his brother until he could set up a barbershop. He wrote: "It's me or that woman. Make your choice."

That was the last summer at Van Hornesville that I worked for Mrs. Rawlings. I left her after that, in the spring of 1950, and never went back. I went to New York and tried to make another go with Bernard. We rented a small downstairs apartment in his brother Jimmy's three-level apartment house. It wasn't too far from where my old room was, where I stayed with Thelma. I rented a booth in a beauty shop, making use of the cosmetology course Mrs. Rawlings had sent me to. Bernard and I couldn't get along. I had bought furniture and couldn't pay it off because Bernard wouldn't help. There was all that work to be had, but Bernard was so lazy! One day I suggested to him, "Bernard, let's do catering work. You know how to serve, and I can cook." Well, we did one or two catering jobs for people I knew over on the Island. But that didn't work out, so I just stayed on at the beauty parlor and did that. It didn't last long; Bernard hadn't changed, and I was tired of being treated badly. Finally, I told Jimmy, "I just can't stay here any longer; I'm not going to stay with Bernard."

Jimmy said, "Idella, I don't blame you. That's my brother, and I can't put him out. We'll just slip you on out." And that's how I left Bernard for good. Jimmy helped me find a place on the other side of town and didn't tell Bernard where I was. I stopped the job at the beauty parlor, so he couldn't find me.

Meanwhile Lil and I got a job at the naval air base, assembling and sorting tools and equipment. This was during the Korean War. Bernard didn't know where I was living until just about the end of my stay in Brooklyn. He found me when I was almost ready to come home to Reddick for Christmas. He came over and said, "I'll take you to the train." Sure enough, he took me to the train station, and the last time I saw Bernard, he was standing on the platform, waving good-bye saying, "I'll see you in two weeks. We're going to get together." I prayed that those doors would hurry and close, and they did. That's when I came back to Florida to stay.

I've always said that Mrs. Rawlings treated me well when she was herself. She would say and do things to protect me. Even in Island Grove, I cannot say that I was treated any differently than anywhere else. People could be heard saying, "Oh, that's Miss Rawlings' girl."

Whenever we rode together in her car, she would tell me, "Idella, ride up here with me. I don't know why you people always get in the back." Well, of course she knew why, but as long as there was no one else riding, I always rode up front. For me to hear this white woman, who was an author and a rich, well-known one at that, say to me to "come ride up front with her" had me believing she was different from others of her race. Many times I have said that I wish that Mrs. Rawlings had lived to see integration, because I believed her feelings about blacks were different from most people's.

It was only after her death, and reading her letters, that I learned what must have been her true feelings, which she had kept well hidden from me. In her letters she referred to blacks as "niggers" and said things like, "All blacks are undependable." She wrote unkind things about 'Geechee, her former maid, saying that 'Geechee was the ugliest Negro she had ever seen. She said many not-so-nice things about me too, all the while calling me her "God-sent maid from Reddick."

Was she a racist? Not consciously, I think. She was a product of the times she lived in. I noticed that she used different terms in her letters for different classes of blacks. 'Geechee, the Mickenses, and other so-called lower-class or uneducated blacks she referred to as "niggers" or "darkies." I guess she considered me a "middle-class" black, for I was called her "colored maid," a more polite term. Then her friend, the black writer Zora Neale Hurston, who was higher up in her estimation, was referred to as a "Negress." I don't know what went on in her mind, but that's the way it was.

I've been called each of those terms to my face at one time or another. It didn't matter; we were used to it. I can't say that I was ever offended—just scared. I remember once in Ocala, when Mrs. Rawlings wanted me to go with her to the movies, she went in ahead while I parked the car. The man at the ticket booth said, "What you want, nigger?" for blacks weren't allowed into the theater until after six o'clock. It just made me scared, that's all. Ocala was hometown; it was worse in other parts of the South, especially on our trips to Van Hornesville. In those days, believe it or not, whites would do anything to you. If you didn't have a white person with you to defend you, you were in trouble. And Mrs. Rawlings always protected me in those situations.

After a group presentation recently, where there were people from all over the United States, a lady stopped me outside the hotel and said, "Idella, how can you still say that you love Mrs. Rawlings?"

I smiled and said, "Yes, I love her still, because I can find no hate for anyone no matter what they do to me or have done in the past." She had been very generous to me, and even sent me to beauty school when I said I would like to, which provided me with a livelihood for many years after I left her. I told the lady that Mrs. Rawlings never said any of those unkind things about blacks to me or in my presence, and I'm sure she never intended that her letters would get into my hands. I do think that Mrs. Rawlings wanted only for her story to sound good, or be what the readers wanted, whether she was writing a novel or a letter. In my imagination I can see her still, puffing on that Lucky Strike cigarette, or stopping to turn that brown paper bag up to her mouth, or balling up wads of paper and throwing them on the floor, then starting to write all over again. Yes, I was hurt at first. I cried as I read her letters the first time, saying, "Mrs. Rawlings! I just don't believe

Marjorie Kinnan Rawlings as she appeared in 1953, a few months before she died of a cerebral hemorrhage. Photo by Carl Van Vecten, used at the Marjorie Kinnan Rawlings Collection, Department of Special Collections, George A. Smathers Libraries, University of Florida.

it!" She never showed any signs of racism toward me, and I have forgiven her for the things she wrote about me. Today, I actually enjoy rereading those letters written about other people and me. Her letters read just like a story and were always so humorous.

She was one of Florida's best writers, I think, but she died so young. At age fifty-four, not long after I left her, she must have felt that her time was winding up. She was well aware of her health problems. She would take sick at any time and have to go to the hospital. She would stay awhile, and then get right back to her typewriter to write another story or catch up with her fan mail. The excessive drinking was taking its toll. I had done all I could to help her, but there comes a time when one has to look out for what's best for oneself. I had left her three long times, and twice she had persuaded me to come back. By the time she died suddenly at the age of fifty-seven, I had started another life.

CHAPTER 7

Mr. Baskin

A BOUT Mr. Baskin, Mrs. Rawlings' second husband, one never does hear too much, for he was a quiet, soft-spoken person, quite different from his wife. (She was divorced from her first husband, Charles Rawlings, when I began working at Cross Creek.) He had well-groomed, wavy blonde hair, and every day he was neatly dressed. In his gentle way he could make you laugh, or in other ways say something that would make you pay attention to what was going on. He got joy out of entertaining others, and he liked telling stories or jokes. He was kind and tried to please everyone.

Mr. Baskin mostly told stories about himself. He grew up in Union Springs, Alabama; his school was not far from Tuskegee Institute. When he told his friends that, they would laugh and ask him if he went to that black school. (Tuskegee Institute is one of the nation's top schools for black students.) This was a long time before integration. I guess his friends wondered about a man who was so close to blacks and so at ease talking about them. He employed a black couple from his hometown, Lelia and W. D. Wil-

Norton Baskin about 1940. Neatly dressed, with wavy
blond hair, he got joy out of entertaining and loved to tell
stories and jokes. Photo courtesy of the Marjorie Kinnan
Rawlings Collection, Department of Special Collections,
George A. Smathers Libraries, University of Florida.

liams, while he was the manager of the Marion Hotel in Ocala,
Florida, and later brought them with him to St. Augustine. I have
oftentimes wondered what was so funny to Mr. Baskin's friends
about him living or attending school near a school for blacks. Mr.
Baskin, during the years I knew him, did not seem to share those
feelings concerning the blacks, unless—like Mrs. Rawlings did—
he could hide his feelings around me and other blacks behind his
always lovely smile.

In 1933, Mr. Baskin became manager of the Marion Hotel in
Ocala. This is the time I first came to know him, as many times
during their courtship I would have to drive Mrs. Rawlings to the
front of this hotel. She was in love with "Norton," as she called

Idella often drove Mrs. Rawlings to the front of the Marion Hotel in Ocala, where Norton Baskin was manager, during their courtship. Photo courtesy of the Florida State Archives.

A party at Cross Creek. "Aunt Ida" Tarrant (*seated, far left*) often accompanied Mr. Baskin (*standing, center*) whenever he visited Mrs. Rawlings at Cross Creek. Photo courtesy of the Marjorie Kinnan Rawlings Collection, Department of Special Collections, George A. Smathers Libraries, University of Florida.

him. We would have to visit her "Aunt Ida" Tarrant, actually Charles Rawlings' aunt. She lived in a one-bedroom cottage on Eighth Street in Ocala, where I would make dinner for them. Mrs. Tarrant was a little lady, short but not too heavy. She dressed very neatly, like a person with a lot of money. She would always have her gloves on and carry her pocketbook whenever she went out.

When the Marion Hotel was renovated and painted gray some years ago, and it looked so tall and nice, I told Mr. Baskin, "I just wish you could come over and see your hotel," for this is how he always referred to it.

Seldom during their courtship did Mr. Baskin come to the house at Cross Creek by himself. Usually, Mrs. Tarrant was with him. Everyone called her Aunt Ida, and she was there often, as far as I can remember, whenever he came to Cross Creek for lunch or dinner. Mrs. Rawlings was always happy to see him whenever he would come. It was obvious that she was in love with him, but his feelings weren't so obvious. He didn't act like a lover or show his love like you would expect a man to toward a lady.

If Mr. Baskin spent the night at the Creek, Mrs. Rawlings had him sleep in the room across the hall leading to the living room. One morning, after spending the night there, he jokingly asked if the mattress was made of corn shucks.

"No sir," said Miss Martha. "We teased up good moss and made that bed for Mrs. Rawlings' guests."

Now, did he laugh. You see, those were the days before Mrs. Rawlings had gotten around to buying new furniture for the house. Later, she let him sleep in the twin bed near the bathroom.

If Aunt Ida wasn't with him when he visited the Creek, Mr. Baskin would bring his two friends, Mr. Bob Camp and Mr. Cecil Clark, for an evening of dinner and fun. Miss Martha and the others would be called to come up and sing as Henry played the guitar. Everyone would be given drinks of store-bought liquor. These were some excited people, and boy, could they sing! Mr. Baskin liked Martha, and Martha in turn just loved Mr. Baskin. I can see her now with that dip of snuff in her mouth, saying, "Now Mr. Baskin, how you doing? Mrs. Rawlings is there, doing pretty good. She hasn't been sick for a long time."

He said, smiling, "I'm glad."

I would say to myself, My, how could anyone give out so much unasked for information?

This type of visitation at Aunt Ida's or at Cross Creek continued until they finally married on October 27, 1941. I didn't know anything about the wedding ahead of time. The only thing I remember is when they came in together on the porch at Cross Creek afterwards, Mrs. Rawlings said, "We're married. Now, I'm Baskin, you can't call me Rawlings any more. You have to say Baskin; we're married!"

In 1941, after he and Mrs. Rawlings married, Mr. Baskin bought the Castle Warden Hotel in St. Augustine. The building, which is now the Ripley's Believe It or Not Museum, is just outside the gates of St. Augustine in view of the Matanzas River, part of the Intracoastal Waterway. Mr. Baskin made that building into one of the nicest hotels in St. Augustine, including a lovely penthouse overlooking the river, where they lived.

Mr. Baskin brought Lelia and W. D. Williams, the black couple who worked for him in Ocala, to St. Augustine as soon as he opened the hotel. W. D. worked as a bar attendant at Castle Warden.

I asked Mr. Baskin if my brother E. M. could work part-time at the hotel to help pay for his board while he was in school. Mr. Baskin kindly gave him a job as the night clerk for the hotel. E. M. would have to walk or hitchhike to the hotel.

One night, E. M. was very tired, and at midnight he locked the hotel door and went to sleep. Mr. Baskin had been looking for a woman who had a reservation for the night. The hotel was supposed to remain open all night. The woman came but could not get in, and went to another hotel.

The next morning she called Mr. Baskin, cursing and telling him how she felt about his hotel. Now, I can't tell you exactly what Mr. Baskin said to E.M. that afternoon, because I wasn't there listening, but I do know from what E. M. told me that the air was probably blue with Mr. Baskin's words. In no uncertain terms he told E. M. that it better not happen again, or he sure enough wouldn't work there anymore. From that day on, the doors of Castle Warden were kept open. E. M. continued to work there until he left for the Army. He quit school to go to New York when

The former Castle Warden Hotel in St. Augustine, showing the penthouse apartment where Mr. Baskin and Mrs. Rawlings lived after their marriage.

he was drafted into the Army during World War II. He was sent overseas, came back once on furlough, but was killed when he went back.

Mr. Baskin hoped that Mrs. Rawlings would be happy with the change in living style after they married, and be content to do her writing in the penthouse at Castle Warden, but this arrangement did not last long. Mrs. Rawlings tried hard, it seemed at first, to make her husband happy. It meant she would have to, at times, get dressed for the evening and go downstairs to the dining room to meet and entertain guests. I say that while he was a city man, Mrs. Rawlings was a country woman at heart, and this was just not for her.

At any time, Mrs. Rawlings would have me get her things and pick her up, and we would go to her cottage at Crescent Beach. Sometimes it would be just for the night, or at other times it would be for weeks.

Mr. Baskin served for a short time in the service during the war. He volunteered in the American Field Service and drove an ambulance in India and Burma for a year-and-a-half. He took sick with amoebic dysentery, however, and came home before the war was over. He was flown out first to a British hospital, and then to Calcutta. According to a letter written to a friend on July 21, 1945, Mrs. Rawlings stated that the headquarters in New York had relayed a cable from India, saying that his condition was serious.[1] Soon after that, he was flown on an Army plane to a medical center in New York. Mrs. Rawlings was there with him for a month or more, then took him home to Cross Creek. They stayed out there for the winter and spring.

After he recuperated, Mr. Baskin sold the hotel Castle Warden. He then became the manager of the Dolphin Restaurant at Marineland, and they began living at the Crescent Beach house.

There were good times. Mr. Baskin had a beige Ford sport convertible. It was a pretty car. Most of the time he drove the car with the top down, even when we were at the beach. He and Mrs. Rawlings would ride down to the beach with her hair flying back, and Moe, their bird dog, would be sitting on the back seat.

Mr. Baskin would always toot his horn as they got near the cottage, and I would wave at them. Mr. Baskin enjoyed fun and liveliness, and whenever he could get some time alone with Mrs. Rawlings it always seemed to do them good. Of course, I could tell when things were not going well between them.

Mr. Baskin had the beach house renovated and enlarged, thinking this would make Mrs. Rawlings more comfortable and that she would not mind writing there. To me, this was not the answer to her happiness, for each year she continued to go from place to place. She divided her time between Cross Creek, Van Hornesville, New York, or Crescent Beach.

After I married in 1947, Mrs. Rawlings had Mr. Baskin hire my husband, Bernard, so I could continue to work for her. Bernard would transport help from St. Augustine to Marineland and work in the bar. Bernard was a handsome fellow, but as I mentioned earlier, he wasn't very responsible. Before long he had wrecked two of Mr. Baskin's Jeeps, and Mr. Baskin was getting tired of Bernard. He said Bernard would have to learn.

One afternoon at the beach house—it must have been in 1947—Mrs. Rawlings had gone into St. Augustine to the beauty parlor while Mr. Baskin was resting upstairs. I saw an old black snake, about six feet long. I got out my rifle, which Uncle Nathan had given me, and fired once. Well, when Mr. Baskin heard the shot, he came running down. About halfway down the stairs, he yelled, "Idella, Idella!"

I yelled back, "I got him, I got him!"

He said, "What?"

"I got him, Mr. Baskin, an old black snake."

Mr. Baskin turned back up the stairs and said in disgust, "Oh, hell, Idella, I thought you had killed Bernard."

Mr. Baskin thought that if he let Bernard go, Mrs. Rawlings would have trouble with me. So he let Bernard continue to work for him until Mrs. Rawlings and I started going up to Van Hornesville, New York, every summer. I was staying there with her for longer and longer periods.

Mrs. Rawlings would let me use her car on my days off. She warned me, "Idella, I don't intend for Bernard to ever get behind my wheel, you understand?" But as soon as we were on Highway A1A, Bernard would make me give him the wheel.

In all, Bernard wrecked three Jeeps. After the last, he decided we needed to leave. I told him I couldn't leave—not this year, I would say. I knew Bernard wasn't ambitious, and so I couldn't give up my job.

One day in 1949, when Mrs. Rawlings and I were getting ready to leave for Van Hornesville, Bernard said, "Idella, you make your decision now. Either you go with me or go with Mrs. Rawlings."

Well, well. I went on with Mrs. Rawlings, and Bernard left his job with Mr. Baskin and moved to Brooklyn, New York, to live with his brother and work as a barber.

As it turned out, it wasn't much longer before I left Mrs. Rawlings too. Mrs. Rawlings had wrecked a lot of cars herself, often when I was with her. I couldn't forget the one wreck that broke two of my ribs, about an eighth of an inch from my spine. I was nearly paralyzed. That time Dr. Strange, Mrs. Rawlings' doctor in McIntosh where they took me after the wreck, said, "You're gonna let Margie kill you."

Well, that summer after Bernard left, while Mrs. Rawlings was driving in New York, she swerved as a semi-truck was coming right at us. I was sitting beside her, and I snatched the wheel away just in time, or we both would have been killed. I promised myself right then that if I ever got back to Florida, I would leave Mrs. Rawlings. I didn't tell Mrs. Rawlings my intentions, though.

In October, Mrs. Rawlings, the dog, cat, and I left Van Hornesville in the car to return to Florida. As soon as we got safely home I put my plan into action. I began to secretly send packages of my belongings to Mama, while continuing to work for Mrs. Rawlings through the winter.

When it was almost time to leave for Van Hornesville, in May of 1950, Mrs. Rawlings told me, "You go spend two weeks with Bernard in Brooklyn. Mr. Baskin will drive me up this time." She drove me to the bus station in St. Augustine, where I headed for Reddick. I knew I wasn't going to work for her any more, but I got on the bus without a word about it.

Mrs. Rawlings wrote to ask me when I was coming to Van Hornesville. I wrote back and told her I wasn't. That summer she wrote this in a letter to a friend about my leaving: "I have been in the longest period of depression I can remember, with no euphoria at all to break it. I am afraid that I am stupid enough to let this be because of Idella's having abandoned me when I needed her comfort-making to get my job done."[2]

I went to Brooklyn and stayed with Bernard until that fall of 1950, when we separated, and soon after I returned to Reddick. I haven't seen Bernard since then. I kept in touch with his family, though, and his brother Jimmy called me in 1997 to tell me that Bernard had passed.

When Mrs. Rawlings came back to Florida, she wrote to me saying she wasn't getting any more maids. "I'm waiting for you," she wrote. I never answered her back, but she kept writing. Her last letter told me—(Mrs. Rawlings never asked me if I could; she always told me what to do)—"Meet me at Cross Creek."

I didn't meet her; I was afraid to. People can't understand that and have said to me, "Why were you afraid?" Well, they didn't live through those days. I was black, and blacks lived with a fear of whites. Even knowing Mrs. Rawlings, or maybe because I did know her, I wasn't sure what would happen to me if I went. Even in Reddick there was fear. A white person might strike you or trip you up or anything, just going up and down the street. If you came to two white people talking on the sidewalk, you just had to wait until they finished or go around. I wouldn't dare go through or say, "Pardon me," or "Please let me pass." It was rough back then; it wasn't pleasant. So that was really the reason I wouldn't answer the letter and wouldn't go to Cross Creek to see her.

I didn't hear from her again. Mr. Baskin wrote and told me when she died, and sent the newspaper clipping about her death. That was in 1953. He said, "We'll keep in contact." Ever since her death, Mr. Baskin and I kept in close contact with each other at least once a month, either by mail or phone, until his death on August 15, 1997.

Each time I called him, I would ask him about Moe, Mrs. Rawlings' dog. Mr. Baskin told me that Moe had become old and crippled, but he continued to go to the beach for swims. Then he told me that one night Moe failed to come home. Mr. Baskin said he believed Moe was taken by the waves.

Sometime after Mrs. Rawlings' death, Mr. Baskin sold the beach house in Crescent Beach. I was living in Fort Lauderdale at the time. One day, while I was visiting my family in Reddick, we talked on the phone. Mr. Baskin said, laughter in his voice, "Idella, come over and see my new house." He gave me directions to the house he recently had built at 77 Dolphin Drive, overlooking the Intracoastal Waterway and all of downtown St. Augustine.

Two of my sisters, Thelma Brown and Dorothy Harris, and my cousin, Lillie Wilson, went with me. The four of us got in the car, with me driving, to go see this house. Well, I drove to the address on Dolphin Drive, and thought I was passing the White House as I looked for the front entrance. The front entrance seemed to me to be the back entrance. I passed the house, all white with black

Mr. Baskin was proud of this house he had built after Mrs. Rawlings' death. Located at 77 Dolphin Street, it overlooks the Intracoastal Waterway in St. Augustine.

trim, which I do believe extended most of the block, as we drove to the end of the street. I backed up and did the same thing once more, then decided to back in the south entrance, which I thought had to be the back of the house.

When I got out of the car, I said, "Hello!" very loudly.

Mr. Baskin yelled, "Idella, Idella! Come on in!"

I beckoned to the other girls, and we all went in. Boy, oh boy! What a greeting we had that morning! Mr. Baskin said, "Idella, just think, this is my house. How do you like it?" I guessed he said this because the cottage at Crescent Beach was Mrs. Rawlings' house when they married, as was the house at Cross Creek. This house was his own, and he was proud of it. We started up the stairs as he gave us a grand tour, telling me about each level.

We stopped on a section he called "Cross Creek." There were things from the Creek house on this floor, and it made you think you were there.

The next part, I will always remember, was the "apartment." He said, "Now, Idella, as you know, I have my two sisters here with me." He called them out to meet me, two older ladies, full of smiles. Their apartment was so nice, with everything they needed, so they really did not have to interfere with Mr. Baskin's part of the house. There was a lovely veranda leading from their apartment. They could sit there and see the Matanzas River, the boats going to and fro, and the oyster beds. It was a beautiful view.

As we continued our tour, going down from the sisters' level, we stopped at the top of a flight of stairs. He showed us his room and opened one of his closet doors, exposing a row of gray, beige, and black suits. I looked around from one side to the other, Mr. Baskin smiling and looking at me. I folded my arms, puffed, and said, "Lord, Mr. Baskin."

We both laughed, and he said, "Oh, Idella, go on downstairs." All I can say is that this was a lovely place, and Mr. Baskin enjoyed it.

Every time we talked, he would keep me laughing. I especially remember when he told me of the last red car he bought, in 1988 or 1989. He said, "Idella, I go cruising down the streets, and you should see the girls waving at me."

I always noticed how Mr. Baskin loved and cared for his family. It seemed they were very close. He would remember to have his family share in whatever he was doing. When he became manager of the food-and-bar concession at Marineland, he had his brothers go along with him to help. Then, when his sisters were no longer able to continue living at their home in Union Springs, Alabama, he brought them down to live with him, setting them up in the apartment at his house on Dolphin Drive.

His sisters lived with him until one of them died; then he had to put the other sister in a nursing home. He told me when we talked on the phone that he was sorry, but he could not do any better. Mr. Baskin said he went to the nursing home daily and sat with her, often without exchanging words with her. He laughed as he related that once a strange lady came over and asked him to autograph one of Mrs. Rawlings' books. He smiled and told her that he believed this would be doing Marge an injustice, for he didn't want to take credit for her work. Before he could say another word to the lady, his sister looked up and said, "Norton, I don't know why you can't get 'credit' for this one book when you've been getting cash money from many of the other books. Go ahead and sign the book and take credit."

After the second sister passed, Mr. Baskin said, "Idella, I do miss her each day. Sometimes we didn't talk, but I would be there."

In 1982, Mr. Baskin was called to take a role in the movie *Cross Creek*. He said they were flying him out to California. They were going to make him up to be the character of an old man sitting in a rocking chair in Island Grove. The character would give directions to Mrs. Rawlings after her car broke down as she was first arriving in Cross Creek.

Mr. Baskin took two trips to California at their expense. Laughing, Mr. Baskin said that when he got there, all they did was have him sit, and he thought, Boy, they are going to really make me over.

"Well, Idella, all they did was lift my hair a bit and say, 'Turn around,' and they brushed a little powder or something on my face. They said, 'All right, Mr. Baskin, you are done.' You know how disappointed I was, and then all I had was that one little line in the movie."

We laughed over that. He added, "But they did pay me for this. So now I think that I am going to write me a book."

Last year when we were talking, I asked him, "Mr. Baskin, what is your book about?"

He laughed and said, "It's about you and all the others." We left it at that.

He told me of the battle with Miss Julie's children. Miss Julie was the daughter of Mrs. Rawlings' publisher (Scribner's), and a friend of Mrs. Rawlings. Mrs. Rawlings had apparently given Miss Julie an unpublished manuscript, which Miss Julie's children later found in the attic after her death. They sold the manuscript, which led to a lawsuit with Mr. Baskin. Mr. Baskin lost the case, and this hurt him very much. He told me how upset he was over it. We did not mention it anymore after the battle was over, for it made us both sad.

Then Mr. Baskin's health began to fail. "I am not doing too well today," he would say during our phone call.

Once, he asked me to come and take care of his house. He said, "I have a girl coming in, but you should come on back home and come over here."

In 1988, when he became too feeble to live in his house, he had to move. My father was sick, and as I had told Mr. Baskin of Papa's condition and what we were doing for him, Mr. Baskin said, "Well, Idella, I am moving to a place in Ponte Vedra Beach." He said it was a place for people after they retired.

"They have your doctors there, and there are entertainment places." He told me that his niece was going to take care of the house, but later he said she did not stay long for one reason or another.

He lived first in a patio home, for he was not real sick then, and we could talk and laugh together about many things. One afternoon, as we were talking about how he was adjusting to living there, he said, "Oh, it's nice, Idella. I have a large place, and they let me bring some of my own furniture from my house."

He told me that his old friends, Mr. and Mrs. Drysdale from St. Augustine, were there and that they would still play cards. "You remember them from the Alligator Farm, don't you, Idella?" I didn't remember them, but having them there seemed to make Mr. Baskin happy.

"So you see, it's not too bad," he would say. "You should come over here and get in one of these homes, Idella."

"Mr. Baskin, you know I will never be able to stay in one of those," I told him.

He laughed. "No, Idella, you wouldn't be able to get in one like I have, for I have everything," he said jokingly, "but there are some real cheap places you could get."

Well, we stopped that conversation.

Once when I called and had not talked with him for a long time, he said, "Idella, call me reverse [collect], for we must keep up with each other. Tell me about the house at the Creek. I wish I could get over there more often, but Sally and the girls [the caretakers] are taking real good care of the place. Give my love to them, and why don't you all come over to see me?" Well, we had a date set up to go over and see him sometime in 1992, but then I couldn't go because the caretakers were planning to drive in the Park Service car and only state workers could travel in it.

We seldom talked without mentioning Mrs. Rawlings and something she did. He especially liked to remember her food, which he truly enjoyed. He could never get enough of our cheese grits and Hollandaise sauce over anything green, especially okra.

Once, before I had finished my book *"Perfect Maid,"* we were talking over the phone about some of the things I would put in the book. Mr. Baskin said, "Idella, be sure and tell them of that evening on our way to Van Hornesville, when we had to go to the bathroom."

All of us had gotten out of the car and gone into this little restaurant. Of course, Moe, the dog, was the first one in, and the rest of us followed. When Mrs. Rawlings asked about the bathroom, a big man told her, "Yes, but that nigger can't go."

Boy, what a night that was! Mrs. Rawlings yelled, "Come on, Norton!"

Mr. Baskin said, "But I got to go."

"Oh, no, we are going to the woods." Then Mrs. Rawlings turned to the man and yelled a few curse words at him. She called Moe and we left, hurrying to the nearest woods.

We laughed, remembering, and I said, "Mr. Baskin, I had forgotten about that. I believe it was in Alabama, wasn't it?"

He quickly defended his home state. "Oh, no, it wasn't." Mr. Baskin enjoyed telling jokes and making you laugh.

He was white and I was black, but Mr. Baskin was a friend of mine. In a consent letter for my first book, he wrote: "Idella, you can use my name anywhere and anytime. You know I don't mind you using it, but just don't tell all the bad. Tell some of the good too."

Mr. Baskin became sick many times and would have to be placed in the nursing home at his facility. I continued to call him, but sometimes he couldn't talk because of his illness. I was happy when we were just able to hear each other's voice. He did not have to be told my name when I called, because he knew my voice. In his own way he would say, "I-del-la." No one said my name like Mr. Baskin did.

Mr. Baskin died on August 15, 1997, just after we celebrated what would have been Mrs. Rawlings' 101st birthday all over Alachua County and other parts of Florida. Mrs. Dessie Prescott—Mrs. Rawlings' dear friend—her secretary and I had planned to drive over to Ponte Vedra Beach on Thursday, August fourteenth, to see Mr. Baskin. I had an eye appointment on the nineteenth, and we were trying to go over before my operation for cataracts. When I called to say we would be over, the nurse told me that Mr. Baskin had just taken a turn for the worse. The next morning she called me, saying, "Idella, I have some sad news for you. Mr. Baskin died this morning."

He was buried on August nineteenth, the day I had my eye surgery. I could not attend the burial, but on Monday morning, September 8, 1997, Shirley Nichols, a retired school-board member and fan of both Mrs. Rawlings and Mr. Baskin, came and picked me up. We drove out to the Antioch Cemetery in Island Grove and viewed the places where Mrs. Rawlings, Miss Zelma Cason, and now Mr. Baskin, were buried.

Mr. Baskin had told me about the mistake that was made in directing the morticians to the cemetery where Mrs. Rawlings was to be buried. Apparently they had taken a wrong turn off Route 20 in Hawthorne, going left instead of right; they ended up at the Antioch Cemetery in Island Grove. By then it was too late, for the grave had already been prepared for the burial. He said, "But Idella, I could not stop them and say, 'Hey, this is not the right cemetery.' Oh, well, maybe one day I will have her moved." As a result of the mix-up, Mrs. Rawlings was buried near her friend and later her enemy, Miss Cason. Now Mr. Baskin lies next to Mrs. Rawlings in the cemetery.

After a few minutes at the grave, standing, thinking, and wondering, I said, "Well, Mr. Baskin, here you are with the two of them. It's too bad you did not have time to remove Mrs. Rawlings' body and bury her where she wanted to be buried."

It was a sad day for me. I was with Mrs. Rawlings for ten years and had kept in touch with Mr. Baskin since 1953. To me it was the last chapter of our love, friendship, and communication. As I looked down at the graves in that unshaded place, I thought, The book is closed now, so go to rest.

CHAPTER 8

Unexpected Blessings

A FTER LEAVING Mrs. Rawlings in May of 1950, I went to New York to stay with Bernard. We lived in a little apartment in his brother's house in Brooklyn. I rented a booth in a beauty parlor, where I made use of the cosmetology schooling I had gotten while working for Mrs. Rawlings. It didn't take long to figure out that Bernard was the same lazy man I had married. He didn't have a steady job, and he treated me badly. If I knew then what I know now about domestic abuse, I'd have had him in jail, but in those days women just kept quiet about those things. Bernard was nice looking and could be very charming in front of others, but he acted very ugly to me. We might have a vicious fight in the morning, but that evening, with guests in the house, he would be calling me darling.

I knew the marriage just wasn't going to work out. We separated that fall, and I got myself a room on the other side of Brooklyn. Bernard didn't give up trying to get me to come back. He knew I always went home to Reddick for Christmas. Mama had told us children that no matter where we were we should come home for Christmas, and it had become a family tradition. So Bernard found me and insisted on taking me to the train station. He was using all his charm as he carried my bags into the station. When he waved good-bye, he said, "I'll see you in two weeks." That was the last time I saw him. Bernard wrote to ask me when I was coming, but I didn't ever go back to New York. I wrote to him to say our marriage was over, and he wrote back telling me I was lower than a damn snake. Now every time I see a snake, I think of Bernard, and say to myself, My, that is low.

The family had its reunion at Christmas in Mama and Papa's house. We children were spread out by this time, and the only chance all of us had to get together at the same time was Thanksgiving and Christmas. Hettie was still living in Jacksonville, married to Dr. Mills, a surgeon. She was teaching nurses at Brewster Hospital in Jacksonville. They had no children. Thelma was married to Alva Brown, Jr., and they had a house in Reddick, not too far from Papa's and Mama's. They were both teachers; Thelma was teaching elementary school in Starke, and Alva taught at Howard High School in Ocala. They had one child at that time. Dorothy and her little girl were living at home in Reddick. She was divorced and was working as a nurse at Munroe Hospital in Ocala. Eliza lived with her husband, Arthur Bickers, in Pompano Beach, between West Palm and Fort Lauderdale. They were both teachers and had two children.

After Christmas the families went back to their own homes. For the next few months I stayed at home, helping Mama, but with no other job. I spent a lot of time with my friends, especially one couple, my friend Hester Davis and her boyfriend. We became a threesome, as I went everywhere with them. One day that spring, Hester's boyfriend said to me, "I'm going to get you a boyfriend so you'll leave us alone." By the next Wednesday he had set me up on a blind date.

No one could have convinced me, when I first saw Bus Parker,

Idella in 1950, shortly after leaving Mrs. Rawlings for the last time.

Left to right: Alva C. Brown, Iatrice, Thelma, and
Alva C. II.

The "Thompson girls" in 1955. *Standing, left to right:* Eliza and Idella. *Seated, left to
right:* Dorothy, Thelma, and Hettie.

Bus Parker, Idella's second
husband, in 1945.

that he would soon become my second husband. He was a short
fellow, and my first thought was, Lord no, I won't be seen with
him. We were supposed to go to Gainesville for our date, which
was a big deal in those days, but that didn't persuade me. I pre-
tended I had a terrible headache and didn't go.

Samuel "Bus" Parker owned a shoe repair shop on Pine Street
in Ocala. The shop was closed on Wednesdays, so that's when he
would come and try to get me to go out. I kept resisting and
would arrange to be gone somewhere when I knew he was coming. So Bus had some long visits with Mama, and she soon loved
him. Mama told me, "Idella, I think he's a nice fellow. You should
let him take you out." Of course I did as Mama said (as I've said,
we were taught to obey), I consented to go for a ride with him.

As usual, Mama was right. Bus and I had a short courtship. It was only the second time we went riding that Bus asked, "Will you marry me?"

I was flabbergasted, and protested, "I'm not even divorced."

Bus said, "I'm not asking you that. I'm asking if you'll marry me." Bus took care of my divorce. He brought his lawyer to have the papers drawn up, and it had to be published in the newspaper, since Bernard wasn't around to be served.

A short time later, Bus asked me if I wanted to live in his house in Ocala or find another house. Well, I wouldn't agree to live in Ocala; I wanted to stay in Reddick near Mama and Papa. Bus consented to that and said, "You pick a house." It wasn't long before we found a house I liked on NW 160th Street in Reddick. Mr. Zizzler, a white farmer and businessman who ran a food store in Reddick, owned the three-bedroom house, situated on the edge of five acres of land that was ringed with oak trees. He had recently put the house up for sale. Bus bought it, and had the deed put in both our names. That was just before my birthday in 1952. I showed Mama the deed, which read "Idella Thompson and Samuel Parker," and joked, "Now I've got me a house, I ain't marrying that man."

Mama said, "You're going to get married."

We planned our wedding for a Sunday afternoon in November of 1953. It was to be held at the United Methodist Church, with Reverend Perkins officiating. All of the family and many friends were planning to attend. Well, I changed my mind at the last minute. I really did not want a big wedding with a crowd around. So the morning of the wedding, I stopped by the Methodist church and asked Reverend Perkins if he would just come out to our house after services and marry us there. He agreed, and didn't tell anyone.

So after church, Bus and I were married quietly in the dining room of our house, with just my good friends Hester Davis and her boyfriend as witnesses. Later, when everybody showed up at the church for the wedding, they were told we were at our house. There they all came, wanting to know why, why. Mama was especially angry with me that day, but she soon got over it. We all chatted and had a nice afternoon visiting. After everybody left, Bus and I drove to Ocala, where we spent a nice quiet couple of days at his cousin's house. Then it was time for Bus to go back to work.

Bus had to commute daily from Reddick to his shoe shop in Ocala, but he didn't mind. It wasn't long before he learned to love Reddick and its people. He loved riding through the woods, and enjoyed hunting alone or with his friends whenever he had a day off.

I had always said, "Let me live in a house by the side of the road and just be a friend to mankind." Well, thank goodness, this was certainly granted to me when Bus bought this house. Once, a retired schoolteacher from Fort Lauderdale visited me. She said, "Idella, why not get a piece of cardboard and shape it like a big hand, put it on a string and just let it continue to go up and down, saying, 'Hello,' because all day long you're waving or speaking to someone."

Bus was a wonderful husband and a good provider, but I wanted to work. So he hired some carpenters to convert one of our bedrooms into a beauty parlor, complete with a separate entrance. Soon Idella's Beauty Parlor was open for business.

While Bus had good business sense, I didn't have much, and before long I had customers coming at all times of the day and night for me to do their hair. In his gentle way, Bus put his foot down. He said, "Idella, you're not starving. You don't have to work all these hours. People are sitting on the stoop waiting when I leave in the morning, and others are still here after I come home. You don't run a business like that. What you need is a schedule, with regular business hours."

Idella's "house by the side of the road," where she could sit on the porch and wave to people passing by. It was the house Bus bought for Idella in Reddick when they got married.

So Bus helped me plan my schedule. He said to open at nine, which would give me time to clean up after breakfast, and to set a reasonable time to close, "so you can be nice when I get home. I don't want you working when I'm in the bed."

That arrangement worked well. Customers adapted to the new rules, and Bus and I had more time to spend together, to go to a movie or whatever we wanted.

We lived contentedly for seven and a half years, and so it was a shock when Bus collapsed one morning in Ocala while driving to work. He was taken to Munroe Hospital and later transferred to the closest Veterans' Hospital, which was in Lake City. I drove to Lake City to visit him daily, fully expecting him to recover, for he had never been sick. We didn't have any children, but we talked about adopting one when he got well. Sadly, Bus didn't get well and died a short time later in the hospital. He was buried on September 25, 1960.

After his death, I continued to run my beauty shop, but I had lost some customers when I had to close during Bus's illness.

The Thompson family. *Back row, left to right:* Arthur Bickers (Eliza's husband), Hettie, Alva C. (Thelma's husband), Thelma, Roosevelt (Hettie's husband), Papa with Marcia (Eliza's daughter), Idella, Mama, Dorothy, Joyce Ann (E. M.'s daughter), and Eliza. *Children, in front:* Gail (Eliza's daughter), Alva C. II and Iatrice (Thelma's children), and Gwen (Dorothy's daughter).

Business never did pick up again, to the level it had been before. I filled a lot of my time in the next few years visiting and helping Mama. She was busy taking care of her grandchildren. She had Eliza's two children with her until they were in second grade, when Eliza took them back to live with her in Pompano Beach. Mama also babysat for Thelma's child and for Dorothy's little girl while the mothers worked. I would visit Mama every day and help her with the cooking or washing. Sometimes we would just visit together while Mama worked on one of her quilts or other sewing projects.

I also got involved in the NAACP when it was organized in Ocala in 1963. Frank Pinkston, son of Reverend O. Van Pinkston, was the local leader of the civil rights movement. Meetings were held one or two nights a week at Covenant Baptist Church on West Broadway in Ocala. Representative members from all the area black churches would attend these meetings, and collections were taken in all the churches to support the cause. I remember my friend Emma Jones persuading me to go with her, saying, "Come on, 'Della, let's go, let's go." A few of us women would drive together from Reddick, and we didn't miss a meeting. We held voter registration drives, trying to get more blacks to sign up to vote. I gave talks pleading with area merchants to be fair to us, urging an end to segregation. Marches and sit-ins were orga-

Hettie and Mama with the grandchildren. Mama was always busy helping take care of them.

nized, although I never participated in those and was never involved in any trouble.

The church would always be filled for the meetings. There was some resistance by whites who hung around outside, and the police were always on hand to keep order. Some blacks, too, were happy with the status quo, and didn't support the activities of the NAACP. They were content with separate facilities. Blacks had their own swimming pool and auditorium in west Ocala. The tourist attraction Silver Springs had a separate park for blacks known as Paradise Park. Some people were satisfied with the way things were, but I knew, as did a multitude of others, that separate did not mean equal. That's why we had to support the movement for desegregation. We were fortunate that there wasn't the violence that occurred in other parts of the south, and there were very few arrests. We had no fear about being involved in the movement, but looking back now at how we traveled those roads alone at night, I wonder why we weren't a little afraid.

Then in 1964, just four years after Bus's death, Mama died. She was seventy-one years old and just quietly slipped away one day while sitting on the porch. The loss of the two people I loved most in the world, coming so close together as they did, was just more than I could handle emotionally. Eliza, seeing what a difficult time I was having coping, invited me to come to Pompano Beach for a visit. That was about two months after Mama died. I closed the beauty parlor and left for what was to be a two-week visit.

While I was visiting Eliza, her beautician had to go to the hospital for an operation and needed someone to help in her shop. I needed a change, so when I was asked, I accepted, and the lady turned her shop over to me while she was recovering. I went back to Reddick long enough to close up the house and business. Papa was still working as a box maker in McIntosh, and Thelma was helping look after him, bringing dinner down to his house every evening, so I felt free to go. I got all of my tools and went back to Pompano Beach.

During the six months the owner was recovering, I made a lot of friends and customers, and decided to stay in Pompano Beach. I became well known in church as a speaker for special occasions. I also got involved with the NAACP in Broward County. I met a white beautician named Marie who was interested in integrating her business, for we all knew by then that integration was coming. She suggested I come work with her, since she knew I could do white ladies' hair; I could show her how to do black ladies' hair as well. So we went in together for a while on weekends, but integration never came to her beauty shop. Blacks continued to go to black beauty shops and whites to white beauty shops, and that hasn't changed a whole lot even today.

All the same, it was with great satisfaction that we saw the WHITES ONLY signs come down, and it was a feeling of great accomplishment for those who worked so hard for equal rights. I think Mrs. Rawlings would have approved, in spite of the disparaging remarks she made about blacks in some of her letters. Other letters reveal that she was wrestling with the "Negro question," as she put it, and that in her heart of hearts she sensed the unfairness of segregation.

One day a woman from the school board approached me about teaching a class for unemployed mothers who were on welfare. These women were all black migrant workers. The class was held in an old warehouse building. Its purpose was to prepare the young mothers for housekeeping jobs. I took the teaching position, and by the end of the term was able to place most of the women in jobs.

Word must have gotten around, because while I was still working with the women I was approached again, this time by the supervisor of home economics in Broward County. She wanted me to come to Fort Lauderdale to teach homemaking skills to educable mentally retarded teenagers. I agreed, and for the rest of the term I taught in both places. In the morning I would teach the women from nine to twelve, then drive to Fort Lauderdale—eating lunch on the way—to teach the "EMR" class, as it was labeled, in the afternoon. This was my first experience teaching an integrated class of both black and white children. I kept teaching that class at Melrose Park Center in Fort Lauderdale until 1976.

I remember once when the superintendent came to visit, I spoke up and told him how much better I could teach these students if I had a kitchen and living room to use to train them in homemaking skills. The next year they put in a trailer fixed up

Idella's "migrant class." Idella taught these unemployed mothers housekeeping skills that helped them find jobs and get off welfare.

Idella teaching her EMR class to cook in Fort Lauderdale.

like a house, with a kitchen, dining room, everything a house would have. I taught the students cooking, cleaning, and sewing, and how to interview for a job. I was able to place my students in many kinds of jobs when they finished school, from positions in fast food restaurants to nurses' aides.

It was while I was working there that the reporter from the *Fort Lauderdale Sun Sentinel* came to do an article about my class. She heard me tell my story about working for Marjorie Kinnan Rawlings and wrote about that in her article. She also suggested to me that I should write a book. I guess you could say my life was about to take another turn after that.

After the article came out, I began to get calls. People wanted me to talk to their school, club, or other organization about my experiences with Mrs. Rawlings. Every time I gave a talk it seemed someone would ask me why I didn't write a book. I began to consider it. I started writing notes on scraps of paper whenever I remembered something about those days in Cross Creek. I saved those notes, but did little with them until after I retired from teaching.

I say I retired in 1976, but really my doctor told me I must give up work. With so many demands on my time, I made myself sick. The doctor told me if I didn't get away from the city to a quiet place where I could rest, I was going to have a nervous breakdown. He asked me if there was any place like that where I could go, and of course I knew just the place: home to Reddick.

I went home to my house in Reddick, which had been rented out for some time, and there I stayed. No more driving and no more crowds until I was well again.

In about 1981, I spent a few months visiting and helping out a couple I knew in Boca Raton. While I was there, my sister Dorothy wrote to me that Papa had taken sick and that she needed my help to care for him. Papa had retired from the packinghouse in 1970 when he started going blind. Shortly after that, Dorothy had taken him to live with her at her house in Ocala, and the family house in Reddick was sold to friends of ours from Fort Lauderdale. For many years Papa divided his time between his daughters, staying with Hettie for a while, then with Eliza in Pompano Beach. Thelma often took him for rides around Reddick, describing the sights. But he had been living mainly with Dorothy when he took sick. So I returned to Dorothy's house in Ocala to help take care of Papa.

In 1982, the producers of the movie *Cross Creek* contacted me. They wanted to use me as an example for the actress, Alfre Woodard, who was to play the part of 'Geechee in the movie. They sent her to follow me around and to practice talking like I talk. I took her to Club Charmant in Reddick. Another member of the club, Edna Simmons, befriended her and invited her to church with her. Alfre accepted the invitation, and the next Sunday she arrived at Edna's church, Shady Grove Missionary Baptist, a little after Edna. She told Reverend Mayweathers that she didn't want any fuss made about her being there, but after services she did consent to having her picture taken with Edna. Later, at a

Idella came back to Ocala in 1981 to help Dorothy
take care of Papa when he became sick.

press conference, I asked the producers why they couldn't use my
name in the movie. They told me they were only using people
who were already dead.

In 1985 I sold my house, buying another one near Dorothy in
Ocala. I continued to help Dorothy take care of Papa until he died
in 1990, at the age of 101.

It was after I moved to Ocala that I began to think seriously
about writing a book about my experiences with Mrs. Rawlings.

At the *Cross Creek* movie press conference, Idella asked why she wasn't portrayed in the movie. The producers told her they were only using people who were already dead.

The actress Alfre Woodard with Idella's friend Edna Simmons outside the Shady Grove Baptist Church in 1982. Alfre Woodard played the part of 'Geechee in the movie *Cross Creek* and spent a few days with Idella to learn and practice how she talked.

Reverend Fred Mayweathers, pastor of Shady Grove Baptist Church, where actress Alfre Woodard attended services during the filming of *Cross Creek*.

In 1988, Phil May (the son of Mrs. Rawlings' lawyer) called me from Jacksonville. He and some others were organizing a Marjorie Kinnan Rawlings Society, composed of people who were interested in her writings. He asked me if I would be willing to participate and talk at their meetings. Of course, I said I would.

Papa's 100th birthday celebration, July 1988. *Left to right:* Dorothy, Idella, Thelma, Papa, Hettie, and Eliza.

The first meeting was at the University of Florida in Gainesville. I remember that Sally Morrison, the caretaker of the Rawlings' house in Cross Creek, and I were both on the program in the morning. There I met some writers who had written about Mrs. Rawlings or about life in Florida. I met Kevin McCarthy and Gordon Bigelow, as well as others. They were to become big supporters when I finally did begin to write.

I continued to be in demand as a speaker, and people crowded my talks at Central Florida Community College in Ocala. I told the audience, "I have a story, but I need someone to help me put it together." One listener, Mr. David Cook, a reporter for the *Ocala Star-Banner,* interviewed me and wrote an article for the paper about me. Soon after that I was introduced to a teacher in Reddick, Mary Keating, who helped me write the book *Idella: Marjorie Rawlings' "Perfect Maid,"* which was published in 1992.

Idella signing autographs for her first book, *Idella: Marjorie Rawlings' "Perfect Maid."*

After the book came out, I was sent to various places to promote it and sign autographs. Word spread and soon I started getting calls to speak and autograph books from many places. I remember receiving the "key" to Murfreesboro, Tennessee, after I gave a talk to their literary group. The library had paid all expenses for me to come.

Each year I have attended and participated in the MKR Society's conventions, and I can say that these have been some of the happiest days in my life. They have been held in different places in Florida that Mrs. Rawlings touched, including the St. John's River, Jacksonville, Tampa, Ocala, and twice in St. Augustine. Through my participation I have been recognized often and have received many honors, including a proclamation from the mayor and key to the town of Reddick. At the 1998 MKR Society convention, plans were announced for a historical plaque to be placed on the rooming house where I lived in St. Augustine.

I have been to many places both in and out of state, speaking to groups and signing autographs. I can't begin to recount all the friends I have made, all the letters, news articles, pictures taken, phone calls and invitations I have received. Once I was invited to speak on a radio ministry program produced by the Mount Olive Baptist Church in Fort Lauderdale. Another time, I spoke and autographed books from Mrs. Bethune's front porch at Bethune-Cookman College. I have received fan mail from all over the United States, and one person wrote from Japan, saying my book was being read there. I am grateful to all who have helped me along the way.

Sometime in 1992 or 1993, Phil May had me autographing in Jacksonville after I had spoken to a group there. Some black ladies came up and wanted pictures taken with me. We talked, and I invited them to join the MKR Society. One of the ladies who did was Marsha Phelts, and we became friends. She drove down to

Idella speaking at a convention of the Marjorie Kinnan Rawlings Society after the publication of her first book.

Idella with author Marsha Phelts at the gravesite of Marjorie Kinnan Rawlings.

Reddick to one of my birthday parties. She also came to Cross Creek when I spoke there, and she participated by reading for a gathering of children from Mrs. Rawlings' story, *Secret River*. She was a very good reader. She told me she wanted to write a book about the black beach in Jacksonville and questioned me about how I got started. We corresponded often, as I encouraged her in her writing. She sent me samples of her writing to read and advise her about. I put her in touch with my publisher, the University Press of Florida in Gainesville. She would call me each step of the way, and finally she called with the news that the manuscript had been accepted. Her book, *An American Beach for African Americans*, was published in June of 1997. I was pleased to have been able to help get her started.

In 1993, my sisters and I had what I would describe as our most memorable Christmas reunion ever. We were all single again, Thelma having just lost her husband, Alva, the first of December. We hadn't been together—just the five Thompson girls—since we were children, before Hettie went to live with Aunt Olive.

Dorothy's daughter, Gwendolyn, and her husband, Ralph Everett, had invited us all to come to their home in Alexandria, Virginia, for Christmas. Ralph knew that at least some of us old ladies never intended to get on an airplane, and none of us were able to make the long trip by car, so he had train tickets sent to us, which we could not refuse.

We are all proud of Gwendolyn's accomplishments. She has a master's degree in art from Howard University and is finishing up her doctorate in education at George Mason University. She works as a collections research coordinator at the National Museum of American Art in Washington, D.C. and is the author of two books, *Lil' Sis and Uncle Willie* and *John Brown: One Man Against Slavery*.

Don't you know we were excited! I was seventy-nine years old, and so we were all up there in age. We had never had the opportunity to take a trip together before, and Thelma and I were the only ones who had ever seen snow, other than the spittin' kind we get every once in a while in Florida.

Four of us sisters would board the train in Ocala the day before Christmas, and Hettie was to be picked up when the train stopped in Jacksonville. Hettie is very excitable, and I had a time convincing her she was well enough to make the trip; but on that morning

Dressed for a winter train ride, the five sisters have a Christmas reunion in 1993 at the home of Dorothy's daughter in Virginia. (*Left to right*) Idella, Dorothy, Eliza, Thelma, Hettie.

when I called her, she was ready. "What?" she said. "You are not at the train station? The train is due there at 2 P.M." This call was made around ten o'clock in the morning.

You would have to know Hettie to appreciate this. Hettie is a person who likes to be ready hours ahead of time; she doesn't like to be late. I'm sure her friend Mr. Hammond, who was taking her to the station, had a time driving on the interstate listening to Hettie fuss and fidget. I just don't want the train to leave me, I can imagine her saying.

On our end in Reddick I'm sure we were equally as nervous. We needed two cars to drive us and all of our luggage to Ocala. One of our volunteer drivers got sick at the last minute, so we had to make two trips with one car. Thelma's daughter Iatrice drove Eliza and me with the luggage on the first trip, then we waited anxiously and seemingly endlessly for the others to arrive. At ten minutes to 2 P.M. we were pacing and fussing, wondering what was taking them so long, when here they came. In walked a whole entourage: Iatrice, with her baby on her hip, and Thelma's grandson, Alva C.; Thelma; Dorothy; and, to our surprise, the Reverend Eugene Broxton and Mr. Philip Samuel of Reddick came to see us off. Reverend Broxton blessed the group with a beautiful prayer. Afterwards he said, "Sister Parker, you must be back in our church on the first Sunday in 1994. We need you."

With that, the real fun began. Four sisters all dressed up in red-and-green Christmas colors got on the train and found our seats. We laughed and reminisced. We told the conductor we had Hettie's ticket over and over again until everyone in our coach was helping us look for our oldest sister when the train arrived in Jacksonville. When the train pulled to a stop in Jacksonville in a

Dorothy, Ralph, Jason, and Gwen on the staircase of their home in Virginia, Christmas 1993.

Thelma's house in Reddick.

drizzling rain, Hettie was the first in line to get on board. The conductor announced, "Well, here is the other sister."

We will all fondly remember the wonderful weeklong visit we had with Gwendolyn, Ralph, and their son Jason. It snowed on Christmas Eve, and we southern ladies had a time walking on the ice when we all went to church Sunday morning. Ralph and Gwendolyn would not let any of us do one thing to help. Ralph cooked and served most of the meals, and they took us sightseeing and visiting all around. It was a grand time we all had.

Today Hettie continues to live alone in her house in Jacksonville. At the age of eighty-five, she stays busy as the senior clerk of the Bethel Baptist Institute. Her adopted daughter, Margaret Ann Mills, is a school bus driver in Ocala. Hettie has three grandchildren.

Thelma still has her house in Reddick, although she has been staying with Dorothy temporarily while she is being treated for Parkinson's disease. Thelma's daughter Iatrice is in the insurance business and lives in Fort Lauderdale. Iatrice has one daughter, Bianca. Thelma's son Alva C., Jr., was killed in an auto accident near North Marion Middle School where he was a teacher. He left two children, Shinique and Alva C. III.

Dorothy lives near me in her house in Ocala. She has also been ill recently, with an illness similar to Thelma's. Both she and Thelma have been receiving nursing care at her home, and Eliza and I have been helping out with meals and other chores. Dorothy's daughter Gwendolyn still lives in Virginia. Dorothy has one grandson.

Eliza still lives in her own home in Pompano Beach, where she retired from the school system. She has two daughters living in Broward County, Cynthia Gail and Marcia, both elementary school teachers. Eliza has eight grandchildren.

My brother E. M., who was killed in the war, also had a daughter he never saw, as I mentioned earlier. Joyce Ann grew up in Reddick with her mother Sadie, under Mama and Papa's watchful eyes. She now lives in Boca Raton and works as a secretary.

From time to time I run into people who come up to me and say, "You taught me." Former students such as Willemina Parker,

E. M.'s daughter, Joyce Ann Prime, in 1992. She lives in Boca Raton and works as a secretary.

who I taught in Gulf Hammock; Pearl Gillis, who I taught at Jacob's Well School; and Johnnie Lee Thompson of Pompano Beach, have kept in touch. Johnnie Lee Thompson was one of the migrant women I taught. She told me, "I'd still be on the street if it hadn't been for you." It warms my heart to know that I have helped the lives of others in some small way.

Since the publication of *Idella: Marjorie Rawlings' "Perfect Maid,"* I have remained active as a public speaker, and have attended numerous book signings. People are still very much interested in the story, and many have asked me to write more. They wanted to hear more about my life, and so I was persuaded to write this second book. I will be eighty-four years old when it is finished. I have had many experiences along the way, both good and bad, but I can say that God has sprinkled my life liberally with unexpected blessings.

CHAPTER 9 »

Reddick, Reddick

OMING INTO Marion County on I-75, you can't help
but notice the splendor of the surrounding countryside.
Hardwood forests give way to shades of green in the
gently rolling pastureland. Harbored within neat lines of wooden
fences, thoroughbreds graze peacefully in the fields as their foals
romp playfully in the shade under stands of ancient pine and oak
trees. You will miss the heart and beauty of Central Florida if you
don't get off the interstate.

Thousands of people do get off the interstate each year and
enter history at McIntosh and Micanopy, where festivals draw
artists and artisans to their "1890 Days." Vendors line their
streets and visitors walk all over town admiring their vintage
homes and churches.

But few people find Reddick, and that's too bad, because they've
missed a precious treasure of unmatched charm and simplicity
that has survived the generations. Coming from the south on
I-75, you can exit on SR 126 and drive north to Reddick on 25A.
Coming from the north, you can exit at SR 318 and drive south to

A canopy of trees covers this road entering Reddick.

The last train passed through Reddick in 1974. This railroad crossing sign is all that remains of a once busy depot.

Reddick, but there is no exit for Reddick. In the 1950s, the state rerouted and widened SR 441. The new road is a few miles east and misses Reddick altogether. Old Dixie highway was renamed 25A or Gainesville Road and is no longer a main north–south route through Reddick. The last train to come through Reddick was in 1974, and the depot has since been moved to a spot north of McIntosh on 441, where it houses an antique shop today. The tracks have been taken up, and the only evidence that remains is a weathered railroad crossing sign standing like a lonely sentinel where the lines once converged just south of the depot.

The change, I'm sure, was devastating to the economy of Reddick, as it is no longer a center of agricultural commerce in the state. But the people of Reddick are as resilient as ever, having weathered difficult times before. Transportation is easier, as most people today have cars. Reddick really hasn't become a so-called bedroom community like many of its neighboring small towns, but many residents do drive to Ocala or Gainesville to work.

The change has also resulted in Reddick's pretty much being left alone, preserving the integrity of the small-town image. Reddick has not suffered from the enormous growth in population that Ocala and other central Florida cities have seen. The beautiful new Reddick-Collier Elementary School provides jobs for many and a quality education for Reddick's children. There are no traffic jams in Reddick, no crowded shopping malls, no huge asphalt parking lots. You can walk down any street in Reddick under a canopy of mighty spreading live oak trees, their branches draped with long swags of Spanish moss swaying gently in the breeze. The roads below are dappled with splashes of sun and shade.

There is a quiet serenity around the old downtown area today. The row of stores is gone, and only a few cement steps leading to empty space are a testament of what was once there. There are no shoppers bustling down the sidewalk, no children chatting on the

The new Reddick-Collier Elementary School provides quality education for Reddick's children today.

benches that were once outside. The green where the depot once stood is empty, except for several stately oaks and the squirrels scurrying around.

Today people gather at the Reddick Supermarket on 25A to shop and socialize. On a recent visit there, I ran into some old friends, and we had a hugging and shouting reunion right there in the store. The manager came out from the back to see what was going on. She said, "I wondered who this person was, with all this carrying on." The store itself is unpretentious, not able and not trying to compete with the mega-supermarkets like Publix and Winn Dixie. The building is small by comparison, but the aisles are neat and well stocked. What sets the store apart is the people. The clerk knows your name; you can get personal service in its excellent meat department. You don't feel like just another anonymous customer when you go there.

People are still friendly in Reddick, and you can get a "Hey, how you doin'?" and a wave from almost anybody you pass. You can stop in at the Reddick Library for a friendly chat with the librarian, Mrs. Fanelli, who still lives in the lovely old rock house across the street. Or you can spend a leisurely afternoon there in

Sidewalk and steps are the only hints left of the bustling downtown shopping district that existed in the 1920s.

This empty green is the site of the Reddick depot. The well pump house still stands in the background.

the cool air-conditioning, browsing through the books and magazines. Children playing in the adjacent old Reddick High School gymnasium come there for a few moments to get out of the summer's heat and get a drink of water. Mrs. Fanelli persuades them to stay awhile, catching their interest with puzzles and books.

It's hard to imagine that the tranquility of this idyllic scene could ever be broken, but it has been. I love Reddick, but, no, it isn't paradise. No place on earth ever will be perfect, and Reddick is no exception.

It must have been in 1989 when I carried part of my first manuscript into my lawyer's office to ask him to look it over and tell me what he thought, for I was about to take it to the publisher. He stood reading, turning page after page; then suddenly he looked at me and asked, "Idella, why is it you say here that Reddick *was* a lovely country town?"

I didn't mean it the way it sounded, I guess. I know that no hometown ever stays the same over many years because changes are inevitable, but to me some of the changes were troubling. Although Reddick is still considered a small, country farming town, big-city crime has visited here, as it has almost every small town in America. Life is not the same for this new generation, and it makes me sad sometimes to think about it.

It's hard for me to describe the pain and despair I felt for my dear hometown the first time I heard on the TV news to "stay tuned for the story of a drug bust in Reddick." The place was near the old Peter Brown's Hall, long since closed, but not far from where Bus and I lived about forty years ago in a quiet part of town. Drugs were not heard of when I was growing up. Oh, sure, there were people we weren't allowed to associate with, but we knew who they were. Back then, we knew everybody who drank too much in Reddick, and we knew who didn't go to church. Today, the ones who get in trouble are apt to be strangers, when there

The Reddick Library provides an afternoon respite on a hot summer's day.

were never any strangers in Reddick before. It's sadder when we find out that the offenders are children who come from a good home, whose parents are well respected in the community.

When I hear of something like this happening in my hometown, it hurts me. It reminds me of the prophet in the Bible who turned his head to the wall, crying, "Jerusalem, Jerusalem," because of the wrongdoings of his people. I, too, want to say, "Reddick, Reddick, what has happened to your pride? Where is the

Children play in the old Reddick High School gymnasium during a summer recreation program.

respect you used to have, for yourself and for others?" But I know in my heart it isn't Reddick; it's the times we live in. These things are happening everywhere today. Because I care about our young people, I struggle to find the answer to this growing problem.

It seems to me that most of the youth have forgotten the teaching of their elders. Young blacks today need to be taught about their culture, their heritage. We have to teach them about the struggles that our forefathers had to go through in order for them to enjoy the opportunities available to them today. We need to help them realize that the rights they have today were not automatic, but came through bloodshed, times of hunger and great sacrifice, hard work, times of fear and running, families staying together through difficult times, and faith in God.

I knew Reddick when blacks and whites were segregated. I lived during the times when blacks dared not go in places marked with the sign WHITES ONLY. We'd heard of the severe punishments and hangings that occurred for those who crossed that race barrier. We knew, for it had been taught to us, that our ancestors had been in slavery for many, many years. We respected the laws of the times, and were not angry, because we appreciated the freedom we did have. Some whites, I am sure, had never thought the day would come when black schoolchildren of Reddick would ride the same bus and attend the same school they did. I can remember when the bus carrying white schoolchildren would pass us as we walked those dusty roads. Not often, but sometimes, they would yell or laugh at us. We blacks never thought that we would be allowed to sit beside a white person while riding on a bus, train, or airplane. No one would ever want to go back to those days, but I am happy to say I have lived through those times and don't regret it, for it is an experience I am able to share with those who are too young to remember.

I was raised in a time when people worked hard to see that their children were educated and brought up in religious, wholesome homes. Our homes were not fancy, not even professionally built, but we were safe behind our unlocked doors. We were taught to work for what we got and not to stand around and wait for the government or others to give us everything. We were taught to have pride and to take responsibility. Each day we were given chores, both inside and outside of the house. I grew up when people, both black and white, cared about the welfare of others, sharing what little they had with those who had less. Today more and more people seem to expect "welfare" to take care of them.

I don't let these concerns spoil my love for Reddick, however, because most of the people I know still hold these values today. It's only a few who stray permanently, but it does seem to be harder to keep families together and on the right path because of all the outside pressures our young people have to face today. I am very proud of the accomplishments of the young people in Reddick who have survived and resisted those influences.

Let me tell you about Reverend Michael Frazier. I often wish my husband, Bus, could have lived to see this grandson of our neighbor, Eva Huggins. Eva and her children used to walk by our house every day. There seemed to be so many children, and they were less fortunate than Bus and I were, so we would help in various ways. We grew to love the family, and I am very proud of all Eva's children. From this family came three ministers of the Gospel. Reverend Frazier has a B.A. degree from Bethune-Cookman College and also attended Gammon Theological Seminary. He was an administrative specialist in the U.S. Armed Forces before he began his ministry. He and his wife have two children. He describes his upbringing this way: "Growing up with a family that placed heavy emphasis on education has made a difference in my life today. So often now, I find myself reflecting on what would have become of me if my mother did not motivate me in her own way to stay in school and strive for excellence. I would be the first to admit that it wasn't easy, and the odds against those

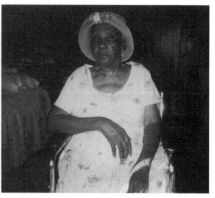

Left: Reddick can be proud of young men like Reverend Michael Frazier, who have overcome odds to achieve success and have given something back to the community.

Above: Eva Huggins, Michael Frazier's grandmother, was Idella and Bus Parker's neighbor in Reddick.

growing up in Reddick seemed overwhelming. However, with a family that believed in me, and a community that helped to nurture and encourage me, I realized that with God on your side you can accomplish anything. For as long as I live I will be indebted to those who went before me."

Until recently, Reverend Frazier was the pastor of one of Ocala's largest churches, the Zion United Methodist Church. A short while ago he accepted a new position at a church in Daytona Beach, and he will be the chaplain at Bethune-Cookman College as well.

When I give talks in the schools today, I try to teach the children about our heritage. I try to bring a message of hope and encouragement for them, the future generation. I tell them that it was hard work that brought about the good changes in America. Needed changes come about when people work to change the laws that are unjust, not break them. I want the children to realize that the educational opportunities that some would waste today were only gained with the effort and determination of those who came before them—people like Blanche Ely, a pioneer black educator, born and raised in Reddick.

Blanche Ely grew up when few blacks in Reddick were able to complete their schooling. She recognized the injustice when blacks were routinely pulled out of school to work as farm laborers. After working her way up the educational ranks, first as a teacher in Marion County, she became the first principal of the Pompano Beach black school. She became determined to increase the educational opportunities for black children, and led a fight to keep the schools open for more months of the year. The community of Pompano Beach eventually got behind her cause, and the length of the school term was increased from November through March. In 1954, a new high school was named Ely High School, in recognition of her contributions to education.

Mrs. Ely did not forget her hometown of Reddick. In those days, not many boys and girls finished high school or went to college. Mrs. Ely helped many Reddick children obtain college scholarships, and she gave many young women from Reddick teaching jobs in Broward County, including my sister, Thelma.

Mrs. Ely was also responsible for starting a migrant housing project, which housed many seasonal workers who came to Florida to work on the farms. Later, she was instrumental in providing a school for migrant children, known as the Project School. During the 1960s, a low-income housing development was named Ely Estates in her honor.

As a result of her hard work as a teacher, principal, and community activist, many improvements were made in education and living conditions for blacks.

I tell the students that I know from personal experience that starting out in life in difficult circumstances doesn't mean your

Ira Stokes credits the loving but firm discipline of his extended family for helping him rise above a difficult beginning to become an honor student.

life will always have to be that way. The same is true today, as it was then. I recently heard from a twenty-four-year-old young man from Reddick who shared with me his experience. When Ira Stokes was born, his mother was an unwed teenager. His elderly great-aunt babysat for him so his mother could finish high school and later college. He credits his aunt's kind and loving but firm discipline for laying the foundation of his life. His grandfather gave him a chance to be a "real boy" by taking him fishing and hunting, and by building things with him. Through the group effort of his family, Ira became an honor student all through school, achieving perfect attendance and receiving many awards for citizenship and athletics. He was the president of his class at North Marion High School and furthered his education at the University of Florida.

He told me that even though he grew up at a time when drugs were available and talked about, he had been taught what to do and what not to do. His extended family stood behind him and saw to it that any foolishness on his part was quickly corrected.

Today, when I visit the schools or speak to other groups, I try to bring that message. I teach that with the right attitude it doesn't matter where you start out. I tell them not to be ashamed of where they come from. Take pride in what you do, no matter how menial the job may seem. I can tell you from experience that even something as simple as housekeeping can be a challenging, fulfilling job, if you care enough to do it well. This is how I felt while working those long, hot days in the kitchen at Cross Creek, and it's how I still feel today. I'm as thankful as anyone else that I no longer have to cook on a wood stove with only a small fan in the kitchen. I can say truthfully, "Thank God those days are over." I appreciate the hard work of people who invented air-conditioning and the many modern conveniences we enjoy today. But the need to work hard didn't disappear with those inventions. That kind of progress wouldn't have happened without education and effort.

So the message I carry to the students is simple: The plan for success is to work hard, study and stay in school, follow instructions, and remember that finding a job is easier than keeping one. Be honest with yourself and with others, always show respect, and most of all, stay out of trouble. Whatever task you are asked to do, do it willingly and to the best of your ability. When you take pride and do your best at a job, you start to enjoy it. If you take this message to heart, there is no limit to what you can accomplish.

And there's no nicer place to accomplish all this than in Reddick. Reddick is not a place to leave from, but a place to come back to. It is a peaceful refuge that beckoned me to return each time I left. It's a place where neighbors are neighborly, kind to each other and concerned for the welfare of all. Reddick is a community where people don't mind getting involved; there is a sense of oneness that you can't find in larger cities.

Reddick's newest post office, 1995.

I still enjoy coming to Reddick, a trip I take from my home in Ocala at least once a week. I still speak on women's day at United Missionary Baptist Church in Reddick. I still get mail there sometimes, sharing my sister Thelma's post office box. Almost everyone I see knows me and greets me like family. When I see a young person I don't recognize, I ask them, "What's your mama's

A walk down any quiet street in Reddick today means hearing only the drone of insects, the chirping of birds, or the occasional laughter of children playing in the distance.

Horses graze peacefully on the site of Mr. Mayo's silo and cornfields in East Reddick.

The road leading to the site of Idella's birthplace hasn't changed much. It is a little wider but just as sandy as it was then.

name?" Then I know who they are, and we can talk together like old friends.

There's an old hymn that begins: "There is a place of quiet rest, near to the heart of God." This is the Reddick I have kept returning to all my life. Stroll around Reddick most any time of day, and the peacefulness that surrounds you is hard to describe. The only sounds that may invade your thoughts are the drone of insects, the chirping of birds, or the occasional shout and laughter of children playing somewhere in the distance. If I listen carefully, I think I can hear the whisper of God in the trees overhead or the voices of my ancestors singing as they worked in the fields. I would have to say to Thomas Wolfe, There are some places where you *can* go home again. I know because I have—time and time again—come home to Reddick.

Notes

Chapter 1. Idella

1. Ott and Chazal, *Ocali Country*, 41–123.

Chapter 2. School Days

1. "A Brief Historical Sketch of Lake McBride School," 9/15/98.
2. Lovell, *Gone with the Hickory Stick*, 128.
3. Ott and Chazal, *Ocali Country*, 91.
4. McCarthy, *Black Florida*, 212–13.
5. McCarthy, *Black Florida*, 74–75.

Chapter 3. Hand-Me-Down Stories

1. "The Confessions of Nat Turner," 7/7/98.
2. "Turner," *Microsoft Encarta 97 Encyclopedia*.
3. Cusick, *Town of Reddick History*, 12.
4. Cusick, *Town of Reddick History*, 28, 30.

Chapter 4. Reddick

1. Cusick, *Town of Reddick History*, 12, 18.
2. Riley, *Marion County History*, 69–70.
3. Riley, *Marion County History*, 70.

Chapter 5. Life with Marjorie Kinnan Rawlings

1. Williams, *Essentials of Nutrition and Diet Therapy*, 443.
2. Bigelow and Monti, *Selected Letters of Marjorie Kinnan Rawlings*, 155–56.
3. *Selected Letters*, 204.
4. *Selected Letters*, 253.
5. Acton, *Invasion of Privacy*, 1.
6. *Selected Letters*, 219.

Chapter 6. Nobody Knows the Trouble I've Seen

1. *Selected Letters*, 219–20.
2. *Selected Letters*, 224.
3. McCarthy, *Black Florida*, 266–67.
4. *Selected Letters*, 11.
5. *Selected Letters*, 257.
6. *Selected Letters*, 275.
7. *Selected Letters*, 291.
8. *Selected Letters*, 305.
9. *Selected Letters*, 325–26.

Chapter 7. Mr. Baskin

1. *Selected Letters*, 270.
2. *Selected Letters*, 354–55.

Bibliography

"A Brief Historical Sketch of Lake McBride School." Website: http://www.leon.k12.fl.us/Public/History/LakeMcBride.html, 9/15/98.

Acton, Patricia Nassif. *Invasion of Privacy.* Gainesville: University Presses of Florida, 1988.

Bigelow, Gordon E., and Laura V. Monti, eds. *Selected Letters of Marjorie Kinnan Rawlings.* Gainesville: University Presses of Florida, 1983.

"The Confessions of Nat Turner." Website: http://www.odur.let.rug.nt/~usa/D/1826–1850/slavery/confeso6.htm, 7/7/98.

Cusick, Joyce E. *Town of Reddick History.* Dunnelon, Fla.: Historic Preservation, 1991.

Lovell, Broward. *Gone with the Hickory Stick: School Days in Marion County, 1845–1960.* Ocala, Fla.: A Bicentennial Publication, 1975.

McCarthy, Kevin M. *Black Florida.* New York: Hippocrene Books, 1995.

Ott, Eloise R., and Louis H. Chazal. *Ocali Country.* Ocala, Fla.: Marion Publishers, 1966.

Riley, Darrell. "Populists and Progressives." In *Marion County History.* Ocala, Fla.: *Star-Banner,* 1997.

"Turner, Nat." *Microsoft Encarta 97 Encyclopedia.* Redmond, Wash.: Microsoft Corporation, 1996.

Williams, Sue Rodwell. *Essentials of Nutrition and Diet Therapy.* St. Louis: Times Mirror/ Mosby College Publishing, 1990.

.